Accolades for *Just E*

"It's exactly what I needed. It shows how to transform anger and frustration into a deeper love and acceptance."
— David Mario, lover of a person with AIDS

"I was moved. The book will be a valuable emotional resource for families of PWAs." — Mike Darnold, TV producer

"I admired how with no extraneous words you shared this most difficult of all human experiences - the death of one's own child. It is a powerful book." — Ilse Gay, counselor

"I felt a lot while reading the book - sadness, pain, loss, love, amazement, despair, anger, joy and gratitude. It was spellbinding." — Elizabeth Killingsworth

"Your story is a celebration of the triumph of love over anguish. The story reads almost like poetry." — Regan Ramberg

"Genuine heart is behind the writing. There is something to be said for a reader being able to feel that." — Bill Diggles

"Thanks for sharing your experience with me. Though our stories are different, the outcome was the same. I know your angels will deliver this book into the hands and hearts of people who need it the most." — Betty Gail Karcher

"A milestone in healing literature. I'm richer for reading it. It touches the heart." — Edie Van Hoose

JUST HOLD ME
WHILE I CRY

JUST HOLD ME
WHILE I CRY

Bobbie Stasey

Elysian Hills
Albuquerque

Elysian Hills
P. O. Box 40693
Albuquerque, NM 87196

Cover art by Doris Steider
Book design by Daniel Stevens
Stargazer lily linedrawings by Frank Ray Stubbs

"A fish cannot drown in water..." from THE ENLIGHTENED HEART translated by Stephen Mitchell. Copyright © 1989 by Stephen Mitchell. Reprinted by permission of HarperCollins Publishers.

"Everywhere I go, I go with love." from LOVE LINES by Joyce Strum. Copyright © 1987 by Joyce Strum. Reprinted by permission of Abundance Unlimited Publishing Co., P.O. Box 4706, Austin, Texas 78765

Library of Congress Cataloging-in-Publication Data

Stasey, Bobbie, 1945-
    Just hold me while I cry / by Bobbie Stasey
        p.   cm.
    ISBN 0-9635589-4-3 (trade paper : $12.95)
    1. Stasey, Jimmy -- Health. 2. AIDS (Disease) -- Patients --
United States -- Biography. 3. AIDS (Disease) -- Patients -- Family
relationships.   I. Title
RC607.A26S698   1993
362.1'9697'920092--dc20
[B]   93-9202
                                                              CIP

JUST HOLD ME WHILE I CRY is available at special discount for educational use by non-profit organizations. For details write Elysian Hills.

Printed by Dataco, a WBC Inc. Co., in Albuquerque, NM, U.S.A.

ISBN 0-9635589-4-3

This book is dedicated to

Jim E. Mitchell

To the life Jimmy shared with his friends and family
To the love he taught us
To the love that continues to live in each of us
To the angels
And in response to the question, "What can I do?"

Preface

Prejudicial attitudes existed among many in our family in 1981 when Jimmy told us he was gay. Seven years later, when AIDS became a part of our lives, each of us was challenged to search deeply within ourselves and examine the darker corners where the narrow parts of our minds lived. We were challenged to let go of guilt and shame — feelings that blocked our ability to receive and give love.

Jimmy spent his adolescent and teenage years hiding who he was, denying his truth to everyone. His fear of telling people he was gay, and later that he had AIDS, was the fear of being treated like a pariah. Fear people would be afraid to be with him. Fear he would be judged and blamed to his death. Fear he would no longer be loved. He found love and acceptance of himself only when he chose to step out of the dark closet of secrecy and lies.

At 18, he involved himself in a community of his gay peers, hoping his heterosexual family and friends would continue to love him and accept him. This acceptance can take time. Or it can happen in the twinkling of an eye.

Even now, more than three years after Jimmy's death, there are family members and acquaintances who cannot accept Jimmy's homosexuality, who choose to keep secret the fact that he died of AIDS. These very same people loved and supported each other and Jimmy as he died, but now seem ashamed of the cause of his death.

I've had difficultly understanding this.

AIDS brought to light the reality that we didn't have time to hang on to old fears, myths and judgements. One by one, I saw individual decisions to choose love surface, gently, like miracles. During the months before Jimmy died, I saw the healing impact those choices for love made in our lives. Choices to love that were not only for Jimmy to make, but for each of us to make. I asked myself, How could anyone return to shame and secrecy about AIDS after what we experienced together?

I believed all of us would be changed forever.

After Jimmy's death, I wrote to friends and family describing the gift of feeling great joy in the midst of devastating loss. I wanted them to know how we took care of him. I wanted them to know he didn't die alone. I wanted them to know that, yes, watching my child die of AIDS was the hardest thing I'd ever do. I wanted them to know how beautiful a conscious death can be. I wanted to share the beauty of our family coming together in Jimmy's dying process, yet I could see that a sentence or two could not possibly convey the clarity of the miracles we lived. How could I talk about the love without sharing details of the terror? I wanted to share this truth with anyone willing to listen: Light is the reward for allowing deep emotional pain to be expressed and released from the body.

I learned from reading and from volunteering with hospice of the possibilities of experiencing unconditional love in death. I learned how my own unresolved grief after the death of my father when I was 14 had controlled and misdirected my life.

I didn't cry for eight years. I didn't begin to heal until I finally let the tears flow.

AIDS was something I had just heard about until it hit our family. AIDS became the proving ground for all I had read: that a human being needs to feel the full range of emotions including the so-called "bad" feelings in order to experience the vastness and purity of spirit, that there is hope in the midst of hopelessness, profound peace in the final moments of a loved one's life.

My hope for this book is that it will encourage a friend, a brother, a dying person to look for and to find the strength available to us all, for the asking. To believe that surely some good can come out of all this pain. To trust in the mystery of God. And to ask someone to please, just listen. And perhaps just hold you while you cry.

— January 6, 1993
Albuquerque

A Fish Cannot Drown In Water

A fish cannot drown in water,
A bird does not fall in air.
In the fire of creation,
Gold does not vanish:
The fire brightens.
Each creature God made
Must live in its own true nature;
How could I resist my nature,
That lives for oneness with God?

Mechthild of Magdeburg
(German visionary & poet 1210 - 1297)
Translated by Jane Hirshfield

List of Characters

Jimmy*   Jim E. Mitchell
Bobbie   Jimmy's mother, narrator of story
Frank   Bobbie's second husband, Jimmy's step-father

Billie   Frank's sister
Bruce   Frank's son
Buddy°   Jimmy's father, Bobbie's first husband
Cathy   Jimmy's step-aunt, sister to Kandi and Ophelia
Griff   Jimmy's step-uncle, Ophelia's brother
Howard   Frank's brother
Jamie*   Jimmy's cousin, Linda's daughter
Kandi   Jimmy's step-aunt, sister to Cathy and Ophelia
Linda   Jimmy's aunt, Bobbie's sister
Lionel   Frank's brother-in-law
Mary   Jimmy's sister-in-law, Stasey's wife
Mee-Ma   Jimmy's step-grandmother, mother to Ophelia,
            Kandi, Cathy, and Griff
Mother   Jimmy's grandmother, Bobbie's Mom
Ophelia°   Jimmy's step-mother, Buddy's second wife
Scarlett   Jimmy's German Shepherd
Stasey   Jimmy's brother, Bobbie's and Buddy's other son

Jimmy's friends: Alicia, Andrew*, Barry, Bobby, Boyd*,
    Bruce*, David, Dennis, Dik, Ed, Elizabeth, Gary,
    John E.*, John M.*, Kenny, Matt, Mike, Peter, Petey,
    Ramon, Ricardo, Rick, Rob, Ronny, Sean, Steve-O,
    Ted°, Tim*, Willie

Bobbie's friends: Florence and Hannes; Pat and Tom;
    Libby, Don and Jessica

Others: Alonzo*, Fergie*, The Honeybees, Laura, Marshall,
    Patrick*, Dr. Ron, Dr. Simpson, Theresa*, Vicky

° not a real name
* now deceased

Jim E. Mitchell

1963 - 1989

Prologue

Jemez Mountains, New Mexico

Thompson Ridge

August 28, 1991

I return to the mountain. I pause at the peak of the ridge preparing myself (I think) to journey down the mere hint of a path to the place where his ashes are, to the boulders where I tossed handfuls of all that remained of his body. I try, unsuccessfully, to crowd out thoughts of hope for a sign.

I choose each step to avoid crushing the wildflowers, glorious this year from rain. I remember how different that other year when pine needles crackled underfoot and bees swarmed before fall's first frost.

I round a bend to a small grove of young aspen, focus my gaze on a thin tree hanging broken in half — lifeless, unmendable — by an elk rubbing velvet from his antlers. One more careful step and the rocks come into view for the first time since my last visit.

Each time I return to this mountain I am struck by how much these ancient boulders remind me of a family. Each boulder, like a family member, is unique. Together they form a beautiful mosaic. The one closest to me is in the perfect shape of an easy chair.

I brush damp needles and windblown soil from its seat. I sit, surprised at how comfortable this natural stone chair feels. It holds me, welcomes me, tells me it will be here for me for as long as I live, and beyond. A gentle breeze whispers the sweet scent of vanilla from the ponderosa pines. Blue piñon jays chase noisily through the treetops. Something scampers under a decomposing log.

Rested now, I relinquish my comforting position, climb around and down the slope to the base of the rock family, peer into the crevice, reach in and touch the dirt. It has remained dry and undisturbed.

I scoop up a small handful to sift through my fingers. Fingers that search for... Yes. In my hand now I hold a tiny fragment. A piece of bone — white, porous — like finding a diamond. If I were a stranger to these rocks, to this crevice, I would not know what I was holding. I might discard it with mild curiosity. But *I know.* I gave birth to this fragment. So, carefully, I replace it in the crevice along with the dirt, and marvel at the other pieces resting within the bosom of these boulders.

Suddenly I am lonely. But then Frank finds me.

"How are you?" my husband softly asks.

"I think I need to cry."

"It's all right if you do. Let me hold you," he says, wrapping his arms gently around me.

I surrender. Slowly the grief begins to emerge. It contracts my diaphragm. Mercifully, I don't have to cry alone. But before the tears flood from my eyes, cries gasp out of my stretched mouth. Pain. The pain. Then the tears.

A minute, maybe two, my sobs subside, my body begins to relax. Although the tears still wet my cheeks, my breathing returns to normal. I lift my head at the exact moment a hawk screams overhead.

The hawk lands, gracefully, on the highest branch of the

tree closest to me. His eyes, big and round, look directly at me. My eyes refuse to move from the hawk's. The tears come again, only now there is laughter in my throat and joy in my heart. I whisper, "Fly free."

He turns his head away... spreads his wings... and soars silently out of my vision.

Ten Years Earlier

Albuquerque, New Mexico

Coming Out
1981

He didn't ask me to lunch very often and there was no way I was going to be late. I hurried in, found him at a glance, even in the middle of a crowded restaurant, even with his back to me: a slender young man dressed to the T's, rayon shirt in muted earth tones buttoned to the collar, no tie.

I waved off the maitre d' with, "I'm with him," and threaded my way to his table. As I approached I caught a glimpse of pleated dark brown slacks. If I knew Jimmy, he'd have on his good leather belt, the one with the snappy brass buckle. His hair was full and thick and somewhere between curly and wavy, the color that was the envy of men and women alike: the deepest auburn, like an October leaf just after the fiery red has faded. He kept his mustache neatly trimmed, twirled the whiskers between his thumb and forefinger to train the corners down. He was fair-skinned, with a hint of freckles sprinkled across the bridge of his nose.

He must have sensed my presence for he stood up, turned around, looked right at me, smiled that crooked smile that made the dimple in his right cheek flash for just a moment. And he winked, green eyes sparkling.

I was proud of him, so proud to be his mother. Now that he'd turned 18, he was filling out, developing muscle from exercising regularly. We played racquetball together, until he got so much better than I was I couldn't give him a good game anymore.

He greeted me with a warm hug. "You look great, Mom. No one in the restaurant would guess you're my mother."

"Gosh," I said. "Thank you, Jimmy." I loved it when he complimented me. He had much better taste than I did, and I knew he wouldn't lie.

He pulled my chair out for me. I nodded, sat down at a table for two.

I noticed a glass of white wine placed on my side of the table. "What's the occasion?" I asked.

"Chardonnay. That's what you like, isn't it?" he said as he sat across from me.

He rested his elbows on the table, clasped his hands at his chin. He seemed extra attentive and I was enjoying it, not trying to figure it out.

"Mom, I think you'd like the fettucini Alfredo. I've had it here before. It's exceptionally good."

My son was ordering my meal. "Great," I said. "My favorite."

"House dressing on the salad, Mom?"

"Sure," I said, realizing how grown-up he sounded.

He motioned for the waiter, ordered for both of us, and when the waiter left, I said: "How's the catering business?" Jimmy worked as a waiter for the Albuquerque Convention Center.

"Last night was really neat. They had a dinner for Gloria Steinem. Some of those famous people are real jerks, but she was nice. Talked to me like I was a real person!"

There was a lull in the conversation, then he said, "Mom,

there's something I want to talk to you about."

"Oh?"

"I've struck up a friendship with an older gentleman. He's been sort of counseling me. We can talk about anything. Anything at all."

I found out later Dik was a role model for Jimmy, a surrogate father figure, a successful interior designer, owner of a nationally known gallery. He showed Jimmy it was possible to live a good life and be open and honest about himself, that he didn't have to live in a closet and pretend to like women as sexual objects.

Knowing Dik as I do now, I can see how he might have said: "Take her to a nice restaurant. Pull her chair out for her. Order her a drink. And tell her the truth." All of which Jimmy did.

"You may not like what I'm about to tell you, Mom, but regardless of what you think, I want you to know that I love you."

I couldn't imagine what he was getting at. "Honey, I love you too."

"Mother. I'm a homosexual," he stated matter-of-factly.

"Oh! That's what all this is about," I said.

"Yeah," Jimmy smiled, then the smile disappeared as he told me: "I was in the fourth grade when I began to recognize I was attracted to boys and not girls. Mom, it was terrible. When we went to church I prayed to God not to make me that way. I remember hiding under the covers and crying, praying...."

(The fourth grade.)

He said: "I don't want to hide anymore. I'm not ashamed of who I am. I want to be honest."

"I'm so sorry you felt that you couldn't tell anyone until now. I think I've always suspected."

"Really?"

"But I couldn't know for sure. Not until you told me."

"Dik was right."

"About what?"

"About telling you, Mom."

"I'm so proud of you, Jimmy. For trusting me. I'm really pleased you're being honest with yourself... (*My son is a homosexual*) ...and honest with me."

It was 1981. We'd been hearing about some mysterious illness killing homosexuals in San Francisco.

A disease is killing homosexuals.

"I'm so relieved, Mom. I'd hoped you'd react like this."

A mysterious disease killing homosexuals.

"But, Jimmy, what about this new virus?"

"Oh, that. It's terrible, isn't it? Don't worry. I'll be careful."

Eight Years Later

He Let Go With Laughter
August 28, 1989

"Expected Death" was a term we had heard used by the doctors, nurses, hospice workers, the Medical Examiner, the mortuary. They used the phrase to distinguish between dying from a terminal illness, such as AIDS, and dying unexpectedly. They used the term to talk about Jimmy's death.

But when death came to Jimmy's body, nothing... *nothing* about it was expected.

It was Monday. The clock read 1:10 in the afternoon. Jimmy lay in his bedroom in his rented hospital bed in a coma. The visiting nurse said it could be any minute. Or it could be days.

His brother Stasey left to go back to work in Texas.

Frank's son, Bruce, came out of the bedroom with tears in his eyes. "I held his hand," he said. "It was so warm. I told him goodbye. I believe he heard me. It's amazing how innocent he looks."

Jimmy's friend Steve-O stopped by after his art class. "I keep thinking he'll wake up. That he's just sleeping." And he, too, left to go now to his job at the law office.

Frank stayed home to edit a twenty-five year old 8-mm home movie of Jimmy as a toddler, then transfer it to video. It's the only piece of footage that shows Jimmy and Stasey and me and Buddy in the same scene — rare footage, for Buddy and I were married only a little over two years, just long enough to have Stasey and Jimmy.

The film shows Jimmy playing in a sandbox that's part of a swing set in the backyard of Buddy's house in Odessa, Texas. Jimmy has one sock on, one sock off, wearing a red-and-white striped romper suit that shows off his curly red hair. He balances on dimpled legs while I brush sand off his diapered bottom, and hold him in my lap on the swing. Stasey is next to me and Jimmy, rocking hard on the teeter-totter with Buddy. Stasey is laughing, charging one-handed, bouncing confidently like a two-year old. Jimmy wanted those childhood pictures shown at his memorial service.

I slipped quietly into Jimmy's room. His step-mother's sister, Kandi, sat by his bed holding his hand watching him breathe. It could be any minute, or it could be days.

I sat on the other side of him, took his hand, watched his abdomen slowly rise and fall. His breathing was quiet now. Barely audible. It had slowed considerably during the past hour. He had stopped breathing with his chest and was breathing with his belly. Laura, his favorite nurse, sat on the sofa at the end of the room, respectfully quiet. All I could hear was Jimmy's slow breath.

Kandi began talking, looking at him but talking to me. She said: "I remember his last visit to Midland. He wasn't feeling well. A cold. Something in his lungs that wouldn't go away." Kandi closed her eyes remembering. "I knew it wasn't a cold. I told him how sorry I was that he had AIDS. That I'd give anything if he didn't. I'll always remember what he said next. He said, 'Yeah, I know. Why couldn't it be something simple. Like maybe the flu.'"

Kandi and I laughed out loud knowing the way Jimmy would have said it, full of boyish charm, without denial, with full acceptance of his fate.

We made eye contact, shared the joy of the moment.

"He made us laugh at things we never dreamed could be laughed about," I said, and looked at Jimmy wanting to see him laughing too, to see that dimple in his right cheek and the sparkle of light in his open green eyes. I looked, but his chest was not moving. No rise and fall. No movement. No sound. No breath. No breath. No, no! *No breath!*

Kandi ran out of the room. I heard her calling: "Frank! Frank! Frank! Frank!"

I watched Laura go up to the bed. Bend over Jimmy. Listen to his chest with her stethoscope.

I heard someone screaming. Realized, *That's my voice screaming!* I wanted closer. The bed rails blocked my way.

Laura was lowering them, asking, "Do you want to get in bed with him?"

"Yes!" I heard my voice say. It sounded far, far away. I climbed in bed. Pressed my head to his chest. Felt the heat, the warmth of his body.

No more fevers now. No more convulsions. No more vomiting. My baby doesn't have to suffer anymore.

"No!" My voice again. "He's dead. He's really dead. My baby is dead."

I covered as much of his body with my own as I could. Feeling his warmth for the last time. Air no longer moved in and out of lungs that once cried so loud.

Laura moved like a ghost, removed the IV, the catheter. Frank came in. Laura left, closed the door behind her, holding out the rest of the world for a while.

Frank draped himself over my shoulders. We held each other, pressed close to Jimmy, cried, together. We stayed like that for what seemed like a long, long time... feeling the heat leave Jimmy's body.

Frank picked me up, carried me to the sofa at the foot of the bed, laid me down, folded my empty arms across my chest. Never again would my arms hold his warm body. *He really did die!*

A whimper on the other side of the closed door. Frank opened it. Scarlett, Jimmy's German shepherd, ran into the room. She went straight to the side of his bed where she always greeted him, the side where he always petted her. She licked his arm, rooted her nose in the palm of his hand, looked at his eyes, whined, sat down, threw back her head. And howled.

Open Door

We had each contributed in the most loving, perfect way, for Jimmy to die at home. The struggle — not only his, but ours — was over. None of us felt there was anything left undone. No question in any of our minds that anything was missing. Whatever Jimmy wanted done was done. We felt complete. Peaceful. Grateful.

Steve-O and Peter placed the phone calls. They took Jimmy's flip-file and my flip-file, told everyone that Jimmy's body would be at the house until ten p.m. and that everyone was welcome to come. Jimmy moved back with us twelve weeks ago when it became painfully obvious he could no longer live by himself. Ronny and Howard sorted and packed Jimmy's personal belongings, while Kenny, Peter, Steve-O, Bruce and Frank loaded Ronny's pickup and moved Jimmy's things from his apartment to our house. We set up our guest room and made it Jimmy's room. Ever since then, his friends were free to call the house anytime, free to visit anytime. That wasn't about to change just because he was dead.

I remember taking people by the hand, walking with them back to his room to see him without IVs, without catheters. To see fresh flowers and lit candles in the bedroom instead of stacks of medical supplies. We wanted everyone to have an opportunity to see him out of pajama bottoms and once again dressed in his classy casuals. We wanted to give them an opportunity to sit with him, quietly, privately if they wanted, for as long as they wanted. To see him at peace and not suffering.

Libby and I had been close friends and neighbors ever since she was pregnant with her daughter, Jessica. Jessica was now eleven years old, and Libby told Jessica our plans to have Jimmy's body at home for a few hours for those who wanted to come see him.

Libby had helped Jimmy's Aunt Kandi and his Aunt Cathy, Laura and Frank prepare Jimmy's body for viewing. Libby was a nurse and a good friend of Jimmy's too. She was the only one Jimmy would allow to catheterize him one night, late, four days before he died, when he was unable to urinate.

Libby said she told Jessica, "You don't have to if you don't want to, but if you want to, you can see Jimmy's body one more time."

"I've never seen a dead person, Mom."

"You can think about it. Whatever you decide will be fine."

The two of them came over that night, hand in hand.

"Jessica." I greeted her with a hug. "I'm glad you're here. Did you come to see Jimmy's body?"

She nodded.

"Are you a little scared?" I asked.

She nodded again.

"It's okay to be scared. Let me say hi to your Mom."

Libby and I gave each other a warm, familiar hug.

"He looks so good in there, Libby. You did a wonderful

job getting him ready."

"How are you doing, Bobbie?" she asked, peering into my eyes, really wanting to know.

"I feel calm. Relieved it's over. I know this won't last, but right now I feel good. Strange, huh?"

"No, not at all."

The doorbell interrupted us. "Excuse me. I'll need to get that. There's food in the dining room, help yourselves. Oh, and Jessica," I said. "Take all the time you need before you see Jimmy."

Ricardo, one of Jimmy's friends from St. Louis, was at the door carrying a single red rose. "Hello, Bobbie," he said, hugging me. "I tried to get here in time, but the plane connections didn't work."

"I'm sorry you missed seeing him alive, but you can still tell him goodbye."

"May I have some time alone with him?"

"Absolutely. I'll show you where he is."

It was like that throughout the afternoon and evening. People coming in, going out, taking their time, hugging each other. The door to his room was open for everyone. Someone would come out onto the back patio and someone else would go inside. People were talking all over the house: Ed and Dennis, who had brought a platter of ham and cheese cubes; Lionel and Billie, paying their respects; Matt and Bobby, Bobby from his Army Reserve meeting still in fatigues and combat boots; David, from the Significant Other's support group, laughing at one of Frank's memories.

Frank was saying: "That's when the shit hit the fan. I told Bobbie, I know he'd change his mind if he'd just get laid by the right kind of woman, maybe a high-priced hooker. And she said, 'Frank, if *you* got laid by just the right kind of man, maybe you'd be homosexual.'"

David laughed, and asked, "And did you?"

Hank, Frank, Jimmy

Frank had his hands in his pockets. He shook his head and smiled, "No, but I saw her point."

I hugged Frank around the waist, stood on tip-toes, gave him a kiss and said, "That was the beginning of Jimmy being able to be himself around you."

Matt pulled me aside, and said: "Bobbie, this is really bothering me. I just need to tell somebody this."

"Oh?"

"I was talking to Jimmy while he could still talk. Just three days ago. I don't understand it. I… we… just he and I in the room. And… and he looked me right in the eye and said… " He stopped remembering and said, "I don't know if I should be telling you this, Bobbie."

"It's okay, Matt. You can tell me."

"Well… Jimmy told me he hated me."

"Hated you?!"

"That's what he said. I was really shocked. I said, 'But why, Jimmy? I love you.' And Jimmy said, 'Because you're going to live. And I'm going to die.'"

Matt started crying. "I don't understand. We were never lovers, but I *do* love him. Why would he hate me?"

I said: "Jimmy could see something about you that you couldn't see. Maybe he could see that you are going to live."

"But why would he say he hated me?"

"I don't know," I answered, and hugged him. "I don't know."

"I can't believe Jimmy hated me."

"Maybe Jimmy felt safe with you," I said. "Safe enough to express his anger about dying."

"What a terrible thing to hear. He had a right to feel angry, but I'm having a real hard time *not* taking it personally."

"I don't know what else to tell you other than I'm glad you've said it out loud, that you've told me."

"I didn't know whether it was the right thing to do to tell you, or that this is the right time...."

Just then Libby and Jessica came up to me. Libby said, "Jessica's ready to go see Jimmy now."

"Matt, is it all right? Do you mind?"

"Go ahead."

I asked Jessica, "Do you want me to go with you?"

"Uh, huh," Jessica said.

"Good," I said. "I want to see him again, too."

I took one of Jessica's hands, Libby the other. We led her to the room. I stood in the doorway while Libby brought her eleven-year old daughter to the foot of Jimmy's bed. They stood quietly a moment looking at Jimmy.

Libby pointed out the items of endearment left on and around his pillow: a button with the earth and a rainbow and the word "Peace," a small quartz crystal shaped like a heart, a white teddy bear, a red rose, a picture of an Indian in a canoe paddling upstream into the sunset. It seemed each time I returned to his room, some new gift had appeared, some new treasure. I never knew who left what.

Libby sat in a chair next to the bed, Jessica sat in her lap.

Libby reached out, touched Jimmy's cheek, his arm, his hand. "He feels very cold," she told Jessica. "His heart isn't pumping blood anymore. See how waxy his skin looks?"

Jessica nodded.

"It feels like wax too. You can touch him if you want."

Jessica touched the back of Jimmy's hand. "He feels so different!" she said, surprised at how unlike a live person the body felt.

I had been surprised too. I'd go back once in awhile to look at him and to touch him and to see the changes his dead body had gone through. Each time I touched him, he felt colder and colder. I noticed, for instance, his jaw had gradually set his mouth into a smile.

He'd fallen in the bathroom just three days before and cut his forehead on the edge of the counter. Now as the blood settled, the gash closed and disappeared. He'd put on some weight before he died. His face and neck and arms and hands didn't show any sign of Kaposi's sarcoma. We saw all this as part of Jimmy's plan to look good when he died.

The first time I walked back to his bedroom after he died, I felt this incredible glow in the room. I saw his bracelet in the cabinet, and heard him say clearly, "Give this to Aunt Kandi." I remember picking the bracelet up, walking out to the patio, waiting for him to tell me exactly when to give it to her. He said, "Now."

I reached across the picnic table, handed it to her and said, "Jimmy told me to give you this."

She started crying, and held it to her breast, then she looked at it, held it between her fingers, slipped it on her wrist and held her wrist to her heart. "It feels like a hug," she said. "I'm feeling a hug from Jimmy."

The day was like that. He could be felt everywhere. His presence was extraordinarily peaceful. His spirit permeated the walls. It was like having one foot in heaven, one foot on earth. The love was that palpable. Everybody who stepped into the space could feel it. What a gift. It made it all worth it.

The love made the pain worthwhile.

The Stretcher

By 10 p.m. all the visitors had gone. Frank, my sister Linda, Kandi and I were in Jimmy's bedroom sipping glasses of wine, marveling at the peace in the room, when the men from the funeral home arrived to remove his body. Jimmy had been dead exactly eight hours and fifty-one minutes.

The men wore black suits, white shirts, black ties and thin rubber gloves. One man was very old, the other young. Neither spoke a word while they pushed the stretcher through the front door. Frank led them through the house, down the hall to where we sat with Jimmy's body. Then he stepped aside to let the two somber men pass.

This was the moment we had dreaded. We had to stand by helplessly, watching his body being removed from our home by strangers, knowing it was the last time he would ever be in this house.

The hall makes a ninety-degree turn into the bedroom. The two men tried to roll the stretcher into the room, but it wouldn't quite fit. It banged against the door frame. Frank grimaced as a paint chip flaked off the wood.

The men folded the legs on the stretcher, turned it on its side, tried to push it through. It still wouldn't fit without moving the bookcase. They stood it on end, tried that. That was the only way it would fit.

I pictured Jimmy's body on the stretcher. What could these two men be thinking? They won't be able to get the stretcher out without standing it on end again!

Then an odd thing happened. Frank and Linda and Kandi and I looked at each other, stifled hysterical giggles at how much these guys with the stretcher looked like characters from a Laurel and Hardy movie. How Jimmy would have loved it and laughed too.

Frank regained control and told them: "No, no, stay out in the hall. We'll carry him out. We'll put him on the stretcher ourselves."

The men looked relieved and stopped struggling, popped the legs back down and stayed with the stretcher out in the hall.

In the bedroom, I took one last look: the white candles continued to burn. The sweet smell of Stargazer lilies filled the air with perfume. His aunts had bathed his body, washed his hair, and dressed him in red socks, no shoes, twill khaki slacks, pink and red-toned plaid shirt with a buttoned-down collar. They'd combed his auburn hair just right. Frank had removed the gold cross I had given Jimmy for his twenty-sixth birthday just twenty-two days ago, and put it back around my neck. Jimmy's hands rested one on top of the other. The plain silver bracelet he had worn everyday for years around his right wrist was now on Kandi's wrist. On his left wrist, three woven friendship bracelets. Petey had given him one. I never knew who gave him the other two. Jimmy had promised to wear them until they frayed and fell off.

Frank said, "I'll get his shoulders."

"Okay, I'll get his hips," Linda said.

Kandi said, "I'll get his legs."

"That leaves his head for me," I said, and thought, *Good, I want to hold his head.*

Our plan was to scoop him up in our loving arms and place him gracefully out on the stretcher. But his body was heavier than any of us imagined. Linda tried to get a better grip on his hips and propped her knee under him. Kandi dropped one of his legs. Frank huffed under the strain of trying to hold him nearly all by himself.

The incongruity of the scene split me emotionally. We were carrying my dead son's body yet I desperately wanted to laugh. How could this be funny? We didn't expect him to weigh anything, but here we were dropping body parts. In spite of the solemnness, maybe because of it, giggles spurted through my lips. Frank looked at me and grinned. Linda grunted. I heard Kandi say, "Jimmy, you're not helping us." We all relaxed a bit.

We got Jimmy out to the hall, lifted him up on the waiting stretcher. The two silent men in black took over, strapped him in across the shoulders and again across the thighs. They pulled a black body bag over him. Zipped it from the bottom. From his feet, over his knees. Over his slacks, his shirt, his neck... *(No! Don't cover his face!)* his mouth, his nose, his eyes.

The men wheeled the stretcher down the hall, around the corner, out toward the front door. Frank, Linda, Kandi, and I followed huddled together, holding tightly to each other, taking baby steps, letting the men do their job.

A black body bag on a stretcher. Zipped tight. Going away. Strangers taking his precious body into the night. A white hearse thinly disguised as a station wagon, red ambulance light flashing silent circles in our neighborhood. Now it comes: whimpers… sobs… wailing….

Why didn't the men in black speak?

It Begins

Being Tested
1988

Jimmy lived in St. Louis for a while. He was working for TWA as a flight attendant at the time the union called a strike. (Ironically for better benefits.) But it was up to each flight attendant to decide for himself or herself whether to join the walkout. If Jimmy went out on strike, he'd lose not only a job he loved, but medical insurance he desperately needed. He called me.

"Mom, what do you think I should do?"

"That's a decision you'll have to make yourself, Jimmy. You're the one who has to live with it."

"I know, but what do *you* think?"

"Well, what would it be like to just ignore the strike and go on to work?"

"John and Nancy tried that. When they crossed the picket line, Nancy's car was egged and John's windshield got smashed."

"That's pretty rough."

"And the people they worked with, who they thought were their friends, ignored them. They treated them like they weren't even there."

"Do you think you could tolerate behavior like that if it was directed at you? Could you still enjoy your work?"

"I don't know. It'd be awfully hard to be treated that way. It's what I've had to put up with for being gay."

"That's what I mean. You have to decide what you can live with, Jimmy. I have no idea what it's like to go on strike," I said. But I didn't say the rest of it: Or what it's like to be gay.

That night at dinner I told Frank about Jimmy's call. Frank was upset, "Damn, I wish he wouldn't do that."

"I know."

"How will he get medical insurance?"

Frank was an architect, part-owner of an engineering firm. He always looked years ahead regarding practical matters while I tended to let the future take care of itself. He said, "What if the very worst happens, what then?"

I said: "I don't know. But I'm sure we'll figure something out when the time comes."

Frank just shook his head.

By then, we were afraid Jimmy might be HIV-positive. We had read an article estimating the cost of caring for a person with AIDS could be as high as a quarter of a million dollars. Jimmy was our son and we would see to it that he got the best of care.

Jimmy decided to strike.

Even before the walkout, while he still worked for TWA, he had symptoms that indicated a compromised immune system. A friend referred me to a Dr. Simpson, an expert on HIV, although at the time relatively little was known about it. I called him and we discussed Jimmy's latest maladies: a sty that refused to heal, then a persistent cough, then trouble keeping weight on, then fatigue. Dr. Simpson explained that any one of those symptoms was nothing to be concerned with necessarily, but as they had occurred one after the other, they added up to a *probability* rather than a *possibility* that Jimmy had an HIV infection.

My fear and panic set in. I wanted Jimmy tested for AIDS right away. I wanted the "unknown" removed thinking it would make our lives easier if we knew. If *I* knew. I found out later I was wrong. I was being selfish.

"Don't you think you should be tested, Jimmy?" I said, pushing him.

"I'm not ready, Mom. I'll get tested when I'm ready."

I don't know how many times we had that conversation. Always with the same result.

Then one Saturday night I got a phone call. Jimmy was calling from 30,000 feet. His plane was circling over JFK, awaiting permission to land.

I laughed when he told me where he was calling from. I thought it was just a fun thing to do to pass the time until they could land. Like when he called me on a layover in Akron to tell me the salsa there tasted like catsup and he was hungry for real New Mexican food.

"That's not why I'm calling." He was crying. "I'm scared, Mom. I'm scared. I've broken out in a terrible rash. All over my neck and shoulders. What should I do?" he pleaded. "The passengers can see it on my neck!"

I panicked inside, but knew I had to remain calm and logical for Jimmy. I said: "They don't have any idea what it is either, Honey. You could be having an allergic reaction to something…. (*Please God, let it be an allergic reaction….*) Can you think of anything different you've eaten today?"

"This is not a food rash," he said. "It burns. I took off my tie in the bathroom and unbuttoned my shirt. There's a deep pain to it, Mom."

I couldn't imagine what it could be. I told him: "As soon as you get to a hotel room, run a tubful of hot water and dump some baking soda in it. You do have baking soda."

"I'll get some at the airport drugstore."

"Good. Use the whole box. Soak for at least half an hour. Call a dermatologist as soon as you get back to St. Louis."

"The pilot's announcing we're landing now. I have to hang up," he said. "Mom... I think it could be AIDS."

Static. Then nothing. From far, far away.

I hung up the receiver and collapsed in Frank's arms and cried and cried and cried. Harder than I'd ever cried before. I couldn't let Jimmy know how scared I was, but I *could* let go with Frank.

We'd been going to couples' counseling. I told Frank in front of the counselor, "If Jimmy has AIDS, he'll be the priority in my life, Frank, not you." Even though Frank had been diagnosed with emphysema, I'd learned through my work in Hospice that he could live many years with chronic lung disease. I needed to focus my energy on Jimmy. My time with my son would be shorter than my time with my husband. We talked about it, the three of us. Frank understood and agreed.

Jimmy called back a few days later. "The dermatologist said it was the worst case of shingles he'd ever seen in a person my age."

"Shingles? Did he say what caused it?"

"Oh, some kind of virus or something. He wrote me a prescription. It's a lot better already."

First Occurrence
Friday, March 10th, 1989

For Jimmy, my baby, my son, my joy, my equal,
my teacher, my love. In peace, light and serenity.
Your Mother.

I wrote that inscription in *Love Lines*, a little book by Joyce Strum that I gave him to help him on his journey. I first noticed his use of the book on the morning of March 10th, five and a half months before he died.

I tried calling him several times that Friday morning to find out how his trip to Texas to see his step-family had gone. But each time I called his line was busy.

Then Kandi called me from Midland: "Jimmy wasn't feeling well when he left here. I just now called him to see how he's doing and he sounded disoriented."

"Maybe you woke him up."

"Well, yeah, I did. He said he'd call me back in fifteen minutes. But when he didn't, I called him again."

I still wasn't worried. "So?"

"His words were slurred. He jumped back and forth between thoughts. There were long silences when he didn't speak at all, and when he did, he wasn't coherent."

I wondered what was she trying to tell me. My mind

raced with possible explanations for this.

She said, "I'm afraid he's having a stroke."

I struggled to control the panic that gripped my belly. If I panicked, I might not be able to help Jimmy. Kandi might be mistaken. Jimmy could be just fine.

I needed to hear his voice for myself. I thanked Kandi for calling, hung up, tried Jimmy's number again.

"Jimmy? It's me."

"Mom? Oh. Hi."

"How're ya doing, Honey?"

"Fine. I'm fine, actually."

"Good," I said. He sounded fine. "I was just talking with Kandi. She wanted me to give you a call."

He didn't answer. I said, "Jimmy?"

"Oh. Yeah. Aunt Kandi. I was… We were… Talking. I'm fine. I feel fine."

My heart beat faster. "Honey, do you mind if I come over?"

"No. Sure. If you…. We…. Talking about. Kandi. Aunt Kandi. I'm fine. I just…" He stopped.

I held my breath… listening… trying to understand the reason for his disjointed sentences.

I said, "I'll let Frank know and we'll be right over."

"I'm fine. Really," he said.

I knew he wasn't.

I had to stay in control. I could not give in to the scream trying to crawl up my throat. Frank could get to Jimmy's apartment from the office quicker than I could from home. I called him.

"Frank. Something's wrong with Jimmy. He sounds strange. He's not making sense."

"What do you want me to do?"

"You can get there before I can."

"I'll meet you there." He hung up, was on his way.

Jimmy was in his robe when I got there. In the living room talking with Frank. They were standing face to face. Frank asking him questions. Jimmy had a puzzled look on his face. He didn't notice I'd come into the room.

I interrupted. "Hi, Sweetheart. How are you feeling?" I touched his cheek, looked into his eyes trying to see.

"I'm fine, actually," he said, noticing me for the first time. He snugged the black and green striped robe around his slender body. Scarlett sat by him on the floor whining softly, looking up at him, nervous and confused.

Frank asked, "Has Scarlett been outside yet this morning?"

Jimmy looked at Frank as if considering the question. He finally said, "No. Scarlett's been… she's… outside."

Doesn't he see her sitting by his side?

Pointing to his watch, Frank asked him, "Do you know what time it is, Jim?"

The question scared me. I hoped Jimmy would feel insulted and snap out of it.

"Sure. It's a… a pencil."

I started to laugh — he was teasing Frank for asking such a stupid question — but the laugh stuck in my throat. I heard my heart pounding in my ears. *Hang on! Find out what's happening here!*

I asked him, "Have you taken your medication yet this morning, Honey?"

"I don't think so," he said trying to remember. "It's in the… " He waved vaguely in the direction of the bathroom.

"I'll go take a look. You might be having some kind of a reaction," I said, desperately hoping that's what it was. But I knew, somehow, this was not the result of any medication. *Gently, Bobbie, gently. He must not know how scared you are.*

"Actually," Jimmy said, "I feel fine."

"I can see you do, Honey. But something's not quite right with your thinking process and we need to find out what's causing it. I need to look at your pills."

I stepped into the bathroom, my mind racing: *We have to call the doctor. But it'll be the nurse I talk to first. Leave a message. Then the doctor might return our call. If we're lucky enough to get a call back at all.*

I searched through his medicine cabinet, listening to the way he responded when Frank asked him again if he knew what time it was.

"Oh, sure. It's, uh, let's see. Tuesday. No, wait. It's Saturday."

My eyes blurred with tears as I searched helplessly for what might be causing this. I found deodorant, toothpaste, cologne, a tiny imitation tortoise shell mustache comb, and pill bottles.

Bottles in hand, wiping tears, cramming the panic back down, on the way out my eyes fixed on the affirmations book I'd given him, propped open on the countertop. It read:

Everywhere I go,
I go with Love.

Of all the pages in that little book, he had it turned to a page on love. It reminded me that in the middle of this terror, whatever happened, we were being held in God's love.

I took the pill bottles — an antibiotic for his recurring ear infection, lozenges for the thrush in his mouth, prescription iron tablets — out into the living room to show Jimmy. "Have you taken anything besides these?"

"No," he said. "Only those."

He wasn't acting scared, wasn't in pain. He didn't look confused, yet he had no awareness of his disjointed speech.

He asked, politely, as if nothing was wrong, "Can I fix you both a cup of tea?"

He sounded normal again. *Maybe it passed.*

"Sure," I said. "I'd love a cup of tea, Honey."

Tea was the last thing I wanted, but I wanted to see whether he could accomplish even this simple task.

Frank and I followed him into the kitchen. I watched him while he filled the kettle with water. He seemed normal now. But... but... Had he taken a recreational drug?

"Honey," I said. "I need to ask you a question. It's all right if you did. But we need to know. Did you take something? Something else? Like... LSD?"

"No way! Mother!? Are you *kidding*?!"

That was my last hope for an explanation to his strange behavior. If he wasn't taking drugs, then... *The virus is invading his brain!*

No! Please God, not yet! It's too soon!

First Hospitalization

that afternoon

"Bring him into the Emergency Room right away," the nurse said over the telephone. "No, you can't wait until Monday. Bring him in now."

I wanted Jimmy to be seen by his regular doctor in the Infectious Disease Clinic at University Hospital, but it was late Friday afternoon. The I.D. Clinic was closed after 5 p.m. and on weekends. I had to take him to the ER.

University Hospital is a teaching and public hospital. That meant a complete physical by the interns and the student doctors, then re-evaluation by a physician-in-charge (all strangers) before he'd be admitted. I wished with all my heart that it was Monday and he could be seen by his own doctor.

"Who is the president of the United States?" one of the interns asked Jimmy. Three other student doctors observed.

"What year is it? What's today's date?"

"Can you tell me what's in my hand?" He'd taken a pen out of his white coat pocket and was holding it in front of Jimmy's face.

Jimmy didn't answer any of the rapid-fire questions.

"Can you feel this?" The intern ran the end of the ball-point pen along the bottom of Jimmy's bare foot.

No response.

"Squeeze my fingers as hard as you can," a third student doctor added.

No response.

Another shined a flashlight in each of Jimmy's eyes, saying, "Don't look at the light." It was too late.

In the middle of the third duplication of the very same examination by yet another student doctor, I couldn't stand it anymore. I stepped into the hall. The physician-in-charge followed me out.

"Are you his mother?"

"What's happening? Is he having a stroke?"

"We can't be sure until we run a complete work-up."

I nodded and sighed.

"But I have to tell you what I suspect," he said.

I stopped my eyes from darting as they had been doing for the past three hours. I looked steadily into the doctor's eyes. The noise, the clatter, the confusion of the ER faded away.

"Your son could have a brain tumor," he said.

My knees buckled.

I heard, "Depending on the size of it, he could have from six weeks to three months left to live."

I forced life back into my legs. My face distorted from the fear lurking in my chest. I said: "But you don't know, do you? You're just guessing, aren't you?"

"We'll know more after the MRI and CAT scans. I want you to know the worst possible. So you can prepare yourself."

Prepare myself? The voice in my head screamed. *How am I supposed to "prepare" for my son to die!?*

But I heard myself say, "Thank you, doctor," and the voice in my head ask: *What am I thanking him for? He doesn't even know what he's saying!*

I had to dry my eyes, go back to Jimmy, put on some other face. He needed me to be gentle and hopeful. I asked my angels: *Please don't let him see the fear in my eyes, the panic on my face.*

He lay on the ER gurney. The doctors were all out of the room. I took his hand, put my face close to his, looked into his eyes. He looked peaceful. Whatever was happening in his brain was protecting him from feeling any fear at that moment. For that I was grateful. *Thank you, angels.*

"What's going on, Mom? Did the doctor talk to you?"

He was curious, but not terribly concerned. Maybe it was passing. I knew I couldn't tell him what the doctor had just told me. Not yet. It was important for me that he not feel even a fraction of what I was feeling. I would not scare him unnecessarily.

"They want to do a CAT scan, Honey. And something called an MRI."

"Will it hurt?"

His voice sounded like a little boy's.

"No, Jimmy, it won't. They just want to take a picture of your brain."

"Then can I go home?"

"They won't have the results until a special doctor comes back to work Monday. In the meantime, they want to put you in Intensive Care — (fear flashed across his face for the first time) — just for observation, Honey. They have more nurses there. They'll be able to take better care of you."

"But I don't want to stay in the hospital."

I didn't want him in there either. I didn't want to make him do anything he didn't want to do. I didn't want him feeling as helpless as I felt right then. I said: "It's your choice,

Jimmy. You're an adult. You can walk out of here right now if you want."

He was quiet then, staring at his hands fingering the hem of the worn sheet draped over him. "No," he said. "I guess I should have the tests done. But I don't want them poking me with a bunch of needles."

"The doctors can't do anything to your body without your permission. Remember that."

The Sign

Did I remember everything? Keys? The magazine he asked for? The list of friends who had called about him?

When they called all I could tell them was what I knew. Which wasn't much. I repeated the same few facts over and over. I left the house that morning thinking, worrying, wondering if there had been any change in Jimmy's condition.

On the way to the hospital I passed a red brick church. The church always had a portable sign out front. I drove by needing to read an inspirational message. Instead, it said:

AIDS IS GOD'S PUNISHMENT
TO HOMOSEXUALS

I couldn't believe what I was reading! "NO!" I screamed, pounding my fist on the steering wheel. "How dare they say God is punishing my son! They have no right!"

The rage boiled inside me. My fist hurt. I didn't care. "That's a lie! A goddamn lie! No one has a right to say that!"

I shook uncontrollably. "He doesn't deserve that. No one deserves that! Fuck that church and everyone in it! I hope they burn in hell!"

I was blocks past the church now. Somehow my body knew what to do: *Drive with the traffic. Move at a normal pace. Don't speed. Use the turn signal. Look over your shoulder before changing lanes.*

I glanced at the other drivers. Their eyes looked back impassively, so indifferently.

"Those church people!" I screamed at a car that cut me off. "They're so damned destructive! Teaching hate and guilt! How can that do anyone any good?!"

I had to tell Frank. He'd understand. I swerved into a convenience store's parking lot, slammed on the brakes in front of the phones. I jumped out of the car, stuffed in a quarter, punched the numbers to Frank's private line at work. He answered on the second ring.

"You won't believe the sign they've put up."

"What sign? Who?"

"That church over on Lead Avenue. It's one thing for them to say that in the privacy of their own church. But to foist it off on the unsuspecting public. It's not right, Frank!"

"What did it say, Bobbie?"

"It says, 'AIDS is God's punishment to homosexuals.'"

"Jesus. It's bad enough to be dying. But to say someone deserves it. That's untenable."

"I don't want Jimmy to see me like this. He'll ask me what's wrong, Frank. I don't want to tell him."

"Someone needs to talk to those dumb bastards. Get that stupid sign down."

"All it does is make people feel hopeless."

"And scared and guilty about being who they are."

"Why would those church people do that? That's not what Jesus was about, was it?"

"No. His message was about love, not fear. And not hate or revenge or anger or control. Or money. But love."

"Why can't they see that? What's… what's wrong with them?" The tears were passing now.

"Are you all right, Bobbie?"

"Yes. Thanks, Frank. I couldn't walk into Jimmy's room carrying all that with me."

"It's okay. Tell Jim I'll be over during lunch. If anything changes, call me. Oh. One more thing. That sign will be down the next time you go by. I promise."

"Frank?"

"What?"

"Be easy with them. They don't know what love is."

Frank told me about his telephone call:

Church: Good morning.

Frank: Who's responsible for the message on the sign in front of your building?

Church: Why? Who wants to know?

Frank: Your sign offends me. I want to speak to whoever is responsible.

Church: Well, all right. That would be me. What bothers you about the sign?

Frank: You have no right to speak for God and say that AIDS is God's punishment for homosexuality. It's judgmental and vicious and insulting to a lot of good people.

Church: We believe AIDS *is* God's punishment for a vile and sick so-called lifestyle. Are you a homosexual, Sir?

Frank: You might ought to ask if I'm a lawyer, not whether I'm homosexual.

Church: Are you a lawyer?

Frank: No, but I have one on the payroll. How would you like it if we filed a class action suit against you personnally, your church, the home church you're affiliated with, and your school?

Church: You can't do that, if you're not a homosexual yourself, I don't think.

Frank: I believe anyone can file a lawsuit against anyone else for anything they want to. If you want to test it, leave that sign up for one more hour, just as it is, and you'll find out if I'm right or if you're right.

Church: That sign professes what we believe. We have freedom of speech in this country and you don't scare me. You haven't even told me who you are.

Frank: I don't care what you believe or what you spout to each other in your own church. What I will not put up with is you foisting off your hangups on the public. I do not want to see that sign the next time I drive past.

Church: Who are you?

Frank: If you want to know who I am, leave the sign up and you can read my name on the summons that the sheriff serves you tomorrow. I suggest you think about it quickly and seriously.

Church: I'll talk to the others.

Frank: You do that. And by the way...

Church: Yes?

Frank: My name is Frank R. Stubbs.

Friendship

"Mom, there isn't even a TV in here!"

Jimmy was complaining about the room. I couldn't help but smile. What a difference from yesterday. I was amazed at the transformation in his mind, his speech, in his energy, stunned at how healthy and normal he seemed to be. I said, "Well, they must've figured if you're in ICU, you're too sick to watch TV."

"And the food's terrible, Mom. They've got me on a liquid diet. The Jello's rubbery. And this broth is the saltiest I've ever tasted."

His words were music to my ears.

He picked a cup up from his tray. "I asked for herbal tea and this is what I get?! You know how I hate coffee."

I smiled at his irritability.

"There's nothing to do," he complained. "And I can't even take a shower."

He tried to sit up in bed, strained against the length of wires taped to his bare chest that hooked him to the EKG monitor on the stand behind him. He made a face. "They glued these wires on, Mom. Didn't even shave the hair. Can you believe it?"

What a delight: machines bleeping happily, nurses scurrying on the other side of the glass-enclosed room, and Jimmy complaining about the lack of amenities. I could tease him again. "It'll be fun when they rip those wires off, won't it?"

"It's not funny, Mom. Kenny's in town for the weekend and I want to see him. I don't want to be stuck in here."

"I know, Honey. What does the doctor say?"

Was it only 24-hours ago that Frank and I were so scared? Trying to talk to him in his apartment?

"They want me to stay until they see the results of the tests on Monday. I'm tired of this. This hospital."

I sank into the chair and drank in his normalcy.

"One good thing, though. They did say they'd be moving me out of this room. I'll have a TV and be able to have more than one visitor at a time."

Frank and I returned to the hospital that evening carrying cartons of Chinese take-out.

"Good! Real food!" Jimmy said, as we came into his new room, a private room in the Neurology Wing. All HIV patients were given private rooms. He pointed to the food untouched on his hospital tray: "Look. What kind of meat is that? It's grey!"

Frank set the little white cartons on Jimmy's bedside table.

"Mmm," Jimmy sighed, inhaling the aroma of pork fried rice and cashew chicken. "Snow peas." He folded back the wire handles and dug in with a plastic fork.

Frank and I smiled at each other seeing Jimmy's appetite return.

"Kenny and Ronny are coming up tonight," Jimmy said between bites. "We're having a party."

"Here?" I laughed.

"Yeah. Around nine."

Jimmy and Ronny and Kenny had been buddies for years. Just because Jimmy was stuck in the hospital with God-knows-what, they weren't going to let that interfere with their play night.

"After visiting hours?" Frank asked.

"You bet. It's a private room, isn't it?" Jimmy said. He saw the concern on Frank's face, and added: "We'll be quiet. What can they do? Throw me out?"

I thought of things a mother should say, reasons why he shouldn't break the rules. I realized I'd react differently if he were hospitalized for anything else. But Jimmy was infected with a deadly virus. What difference would it make if he bent a few hospital rules?

Jimmy said: "Ronny's bringing the *Dream Girls* tape. We heard it at Kenny's in El Paso.... "

Frank and I listened to Jimmy plan his evening as if he hadn't been sick at all. In between bites of Chinese food, Jimmy's eyes shone bright with excitement, full of life, anticipating an evening with friends.

" ...Kenny's bringing the tape player. We won't play it too loud, Frank," Jimmy said. "I wish I had something besides this hospital gown to wear. I can't wait!"

Ophelia, Jimmy's step-mother, asked me one time, "Of all of these young men who come over here, is one of them Jimmy's *special* friend?"

I knew what she meant. I said, "I'd have to say probably Rob."

"Really?" she said. "I would've assumed Kenny."

I was surprised she'd guessed Kenny, tried to see through her eyes why she perceived their relationship that way. Kenny sold cosmetics for a large department store in El Paso. He brought a sackful of samples over to the house one night and gave facials to Ophelia and her sisters, and to me and my sister. We sat around the kitchen table that night, laughed like a family. Kenny was like a brother, or maybe a son. He had a warm and giving heart.

"They're very close friends," I said. "But lovers? I don't think so."

Whenever Kenny was in town to visit his family, he'd stop to see Jimmy too. They'd spend time together, visit friends, go to parties. Kenny wanted to see as many of their friends as he could see while he was in town and he wanted Jimmy to go with him, like he and Ronny and Jimmy always did before Jimmy got sick. Jimmy told me how they had left a party at Ramon's house to go to one at Ronny's brother's. At the second party, Jimmy realized it was time to take his medication and he had forgotten to bring his AZT pills. He was supposed to take them every four hours. Kenny offered to go back to the house and get them. On his way out the door, Kenny turned and shouted (at least it seemed that way to Jimmy): "I'll be back in a few minutes, everyone. I'm going to get Jimmy's AZT." Jimmy had been having such a good time, like in the old days, with no talk about HIV. He said he was afraid everyone would treat him differently if they knew for sure he was infected with HIV. Kenny, on the other hand, genuinely did not think he'd done anything out of line.

There was a line between who was a buddy and who was a dating sexual partner. I had no idea who, if anyone, Jimmy went to bed with. It wasn't my business, but I was curious. I asked one time, "Jimmy, have you and Steve-O ever gone to bed?" Jimmy said, "No, Mother." And I let it go at that.

One night Steve-O brought over a bouquet of roses fresh out of his garden, and a hot macaroni and cheese and ground beef casserole. "I thought I'd visit with Jimmy tonight," he said, "while you and Frank go to your support group." We said hi and bye, that we'd see them in a couple of hours. When we got back, Steve-O was standing outside the bathroom door. We heard him knock and ask, "Are you okay in there, Sugar?" I asked what was wrong, and Steve-O said that he heard Jimmy throw up at the same time he was trying to go to the bathroom. Steve-O went in to help him, waving off our offer to help. He cleaned Jimmy up, put him in fresh clothes, and saw Jimmy comfortably to bed before he left.

Jimmy's friends enriched his life. I could not take their place, nor did I want to. Jimmy needed all the love he could get. So did we. Those same friends who were in his life are in our life now. I learned to know Jimmy through his friends.

The next day at the hospital, I asked Jimmy, "Did you guys have a good time last night?"

"It was great, Mom. We partied till nearly midnight. No one threw us out, either!"

He told me how Kenny and Ronny and he formed a chorus line and shuffled and kicked and side-stepped their way from the foot of the bed, across the room, through the open door and out into the hospital hall. "The back of my hospital gown kept flapping open. I didn't have underwear on!"

"You all must have been quite the sight."

Laughter Dies

After an MRI, a brain scan, a lumbar puncture, an EEG, a Gallium scan, an echocardiogram, a carotid Doppler, and a complete blood work-up, all of which resulted in "normal" or "negative" findings, the doctors discharged Jimmy with a "provisional" diagnosis of possible "Transient Ischemic Attacks" (they called them TIAs for short). They explained that TIAs are interruptions of the blood supply to "certain tissues" and that TIAs "pass with time."

I was at his apartment a few days later helping him sort through, fill out, sign and mail insurance claims when he had the next episode. The TIA began with a numbness in his right hand, a numb so numb he said his hand felt like it belonged to someone else.

"I'm trying to make a fist, but I can't feel my hand," he said, struggling with the words, slowly flexing his fist open and closed. "I'm having trouble holding my head up."

"Do you have a headache?" I asked.

"No. But something funny is happening with my eye. I can see lights," he said, squinching that eye.

"Are they like the floaters you see sometimes drifting across your eyes?"

"Floaters look different. These are flashing lights. And bright. It's wierd."

"Are you in any pain?"

"No. A little… tired, maybe, I guess."

"Why don't you lie down, Sweetie. I think you're having another one of those episodes. It'll pass in a few minutes." Inside, though, I was terrified, watching the change in his body, his personality. He looked so child-like. So innocent.

"Okay. Sure. I feel fine, though. Just a little tired."

"Maybe we should call the doctor," I asked.

"They'll just say to go to the Emergency Room. I don't want to go to the hospital again."

I knew if we did, all they would do is put him through another battery of tests. The last series had proven useless. What good would a new series do? Why would it be any different now?

Jimmy said, "I'll just lie on the sofa until it goes away."

Those weeks following that first hospitalization were, for me, filled with fear of an unknown future. What was happening to his body? To his brain? Why wouldn't the tests show anything? What would it be like if and when the symptoms worsened? Would his whole body just fall asleep one day? Leave him paralyzed? Or worse?

I'd phone him every morning at his apartment, forcing myself to wait until at least eleven, hoping a late call would not wake him. But in spite of the late hour, most days it did.

"Good morning, Sunshine! Were you asleep?" I'd hoped he'd been up for hours, like he used to, ready to face the day with enthusiasm and energy. Do a day trip to Santa Fe with a friend. Maybe plan a dinner party, buy groceries. At least take Scarlett out for a walk.

Scarlett and Jimmy

"I need to get up," he'd say sleepily.

"How're you feeling?"

"A little tired, that's all."

He sounded like the night's sleep hadn't done him any good.

"Go back to sleep. Give me a call when you wake up."

"Thanks, Mom, I'll call you later."

Silence from his end of the line.

I hated interrupting his sleep, but he seemed to be always sleeping. I felt like I wanted more from him. Perhaps a funny story about something he'd done with a friend the night before. A complaint about Scarlett digging in the kitchen trash. Something, anything. Maybe he'd been to the flea market and found the perfect "treasure" for his apartment.

Maybe he'd tell me: "It was only three bucks! Can you imagine that?"

Gradually, little by little, fatigue robbed him — robbed us — of his delightful sense of humor. I needed a pun, a joke. I needed to hear his laughter.

He'd come by the house to do his laundry, with Scarlett tagging behind. He'd sort his whites from his darks, start the first load, then, already exhausted, he'd lie down "for just a few minutes," he'd say.

I'd turn the phones off, finish his laundry, walk Scarlett around the neighborhood, wait for him to wake up.

After a few hours I'd touch him to ask, "Can I get you something to eat?"

"No, thanks," he'd say, his voice still weary. "I'm not hungry."

"Now Jimmy, tell me truthfully, when was the last time you ate?"

"I had something after work last night."

"But it's three in the afternoon, Honey. Let me fix you something. You have to eat."

"Three o'clock? I was supposed to help Petey with his recycling project today."

"What time was that?"

"Around noon. We were going to let Scarlett and Mookie play while we sorted the plastic from the glass."

"You might call and leave a message on his machine. Let him know what happened."

"I will. Later."

"Let me fix you something to eat."

I knew he wasn't hungry, but I went into the kitchen anyway, busied myself making him soup and a sandwich, doing my job as a mother, seeing that my son was fed. As if feeding him would keep him from losing more weight. If he wasn't losing weight, then maybe he wasn't sick. If he ate more, maybe he'd have more energy. If he had more energy, maybe he'd laugh.

God, Jimmy, how I miss hearing you laugh....

Forks

After the test and we knew, for sure, that Jimmy was HIV-positive, there was a period of time when all the knowledge we had armed ourselves with could not dispel the fear that Jimmy would infect us with AIDS.

I hated when the fear popped up, for in those moments the fear separated me from my love for Jimmy.

For instance, on this particular evening, Jimmy had a good appetite and wanted to go out to eat. It'd been a "good day" for him — high energy, talkative, normal. No night sweats the previous night, no earache, no sign of fatigue. He'd held food down for two days, had enough energy to dress, to talk on the phone, to play roll-on-the-floor with Scarlett. He wanted to eat at Scalo's, a Northern Italian hot-spot in the neighborhood.

Going out to fancy restaurants had always been family recreation for us. We would order different entrées and agree to share, to taste as many dishes as possible.

"What are you going to order, Mom?"

I studied the menu. "Oh, let's see. Either the *Linguini alla Amatriciana,* or the *Spagatini con Pollo,*" I said, trying to sound Italian. "Or maybe the pasta special," I added, hoping one of the choices was something he wanted to order too.

"Oh, good," he said. "I think I'll have the linguini."

"Then I'll have the spaghetti. And we can taste, okay?"

"Sure!"

When the meals arrived, he commented on the flair of the waiter, and I admired the presentation of the food.

"Mmm," I said. "Mine looks good."

"Yours does look better than mine. Let me taste."

I held a forkful of my pasta and grilled chicken out toward him and heard: *All he's doing is eating it off my fork. How bad can that be?*

But then the fear slammed into my head: *WHAT ARE YOU DOING? YOU'LL GET AIDS!*

My rational mind tried to talk to the fear. It said: *Don't be silly. That's not how AIDS is transmitted.*

But the fear persisted, louder: *HOW DO YOU KNOW THAT? THE EXPERTS COULD BE WRONG! DON'T BE STUPID! YOU'LL DIE!*

My rational mind stopped it: *That's absurd.*

My mind raced through all the literature and newspaper articles and talks with doctors and professionals. I couldn't find a thing to substantiate this fear.

You're not going to let the fear stop you. You're going to do this anyway.

All of that in the split second between holding the forkful of food out to Jimmy, watching his mouth open, the fork sliding into his mouth. And then my putting the same fork into my mouth with the next bite of food.

To the observer, nothing was different from any other time we'd performed this family ritual. But *I knew* it was different. For one split second. It came and it went.

And I hated it.

Puppies

"Mom, I think I want to have Scarlett bred. I want her to have a litter of puppies."

"Great! That'd be fun!" I crowded out all worrisome thoughts, let myself take in his enthusiasm. His excitement at helping to create new life. I knew he had no idea just how demanding this would be. But if he was willing, so was I.

Jimmy's step-uncle Griff owned a kennel in Midland. Griff bred and sold only German Shepherd dogs, shipping pups all over the world. Jimmy took Scarlett there to be bred. Of all the possible mates, Jimmy chose the strongest-looking male with the sweetest disposition. Three weeks later, he rented a car and made the ten and a half hour drive back to Midland to pick her up.

Back in Albuquerque, he fussed over Scarlett like he would a pregnant wife. He did little things to make her comfortable. He fixed her a bed out of an old blanket, made sure she took her walks. Griff suggested that during the nine-week gestation period she eat raw chicken livers everyday. Jimmy fed her an entire pint thinking if a little was good then a lot must be better. He had to get his carpet cleaned when he couldn't get her outside fast enough.

The weekend came when Jimmy and I were to meet my sister Linda in El Paso for a relaxing two days of shopping and movie-going. Jimmy and his Aunt Linda had always been close. I thought it would be good for him to get away, to stay at a motel, to see something different for a change. He phoned me just as I was leaving the house to pick him up. He said he'd changed his mind about El Paso. His voice sounded strained.

"Are you all right?" I asked him.

"A little tired, that's all."

"Are you sure you don't want to go? I'll do the driving."

"No, it's not that. Frank thinks Scarlett could have her puppies any day now. I don't want to miss it."

I met Linda in El Paso alone.

While I was away, Frank went over to Jimmy's apartment to see how he and Scarlett were doing. Frank's from Tennessee, raised on a farm. He's seen lots of animals being born. He took a look at Scarlett, told Jimmy, "I think you might become a dad tonight."

Together, Frank and Jimmy built a birthing box out of a refrigerator carton they found by a dumpster. They lined the bottom of the box with a scrap of linoleum, covered it with plastic and put Scarlett's pink "blankie" inside.

Frank said, "Maybe she'd be more comfortable at the house. We can put her in the living room. You can sleep on the sofa. Okay?"

They moved Scarlett and the big box over to the house in the back of the Wagoneer.

Jimmy woke Frank up at 4:21 the next morning to tell him that Scarlett was restless. Frank went out to check.

Scarlett was licking herself, already dilated. Frank asked

Jimmy to get the stack of old towels from the garage. The first puppy was born at 4:26.

Scarlett tried to clean each newborn puppy with her tongue, but she was a first-time mother, so Frank finished the job with the clean towels. Griff had told Jimmy to keep track of what order the puppies were born, their weights, and any distinguishing markings, so Jimmy had a pad of paper and a food scale ready. As busy as Frank was, he stopped to take pictures of Jimmy sitting in the rocking chair, spreading the puppies' hind legs checking their sex.

Scarlett had six puppies in all.

Scarlett and her puppies

Jimmy had been up most of the night and was exhausted. He had difficulty concentrating. Later, when we read what he'd written, we couldn't make any sense of his notes.

Jimmy called me at the motel in El Paso Sunday morning. "Mom! She had them!" He sounded so like the proud father.

When I returned, I was greeted by the image of Frank coaxing Scarlett to nurse six puppies in the refrigerator box, now moved to the guest room, while Jimmy watched from the sofa bed, tired but contented.

Jimmy stayed at the house for several days so Frank and I could help with the care of the new mom and her babies. We'd hear a pup squealing in the middle of the night, a sure sign Scarlett was crushing one. Jimmy couldn't wake himself up enough to move the dog, and Frank wound up sleeping in the guest room with the pups.

Over the next six weeks the puppies squealed and yipped and yelped and required lots and lots of attention from me and Frank. Jimmy tried to help as much as he could, but fatigue prevented him from doing much more than cuddling them. I wouldn't have robbed him of the experience for anything. He loved puppies. And babies. And life.

In the mornings I would clean the mess on the floor, feed the puppies their mush and try to encourage Scarlett to let them nurse. Jimmy would come out in his robe, sit in the chair next to their box, scoop up a puppy and press it close to his face feeling the silky, soft baby fur against his cheek. He'd put that one down among the puppies whining at his bare feet, and pick up another. He'd do that until he'd held each one.

I remember telling Jimmy what a good father he would make. He said, "You know, Mom, I've often thought about adopting a child."

I looked at him, and said, "You've never mentioned that before." And I quickly hid the grief that rushed in.

"That's not so much out of the question anymore. You know, I think I would have, too, if it wasn't for…"

Jimmy, a puppy, Bobbie

Buddy's Call

Jimmy mentioned casually, on three different occasions, that he would like to see his dad. I was married to Buddy when we had Jimmy and Stasey. We divorced when the boys were 1½ and 2½. I cared for them myself until they went to live with Buddy and his wife Ophelia, 4½ years later when Jimmy started school. The boys lived with them through high school. Jimmy moved to Albuquerque, moved in with Frank and me, as soon as he graduated.

"Hello, Buddy? It's Bobbie," I said into the phone.

"Oh, hello," he said.

"I want to let you know how Jimmy is."

"Jimmy? When he called last week, he said he was fine."

"He says he's fine. But I need to let you know how he really is."

"I don't understand."

I breathed in slowly. Buddy knew Jimmy was HIV-positive, but I wasn't sure what else he knew. In the silence between my breaths I asked my angels for permission to tell him about the changes in Jimmy's health. I heard a whisper: *Tell Buddy everything.*

"Jimmy's much sicker now."

"How sick can he be?"

"Buddy, AIDS is terminal."

I heard his breath catch on the other end of the line. I said: "He's staying over with us practically every night now. He doesn't have the strength to fix his own meals anymore. He can barely get through a shift at work without lying down."

"What are you asking me to do?" he said in a voice higher than before.

"He needs to see you."

"Why can't he come down here?"

"He's too sick to travel. He needs you to come here."

When he didn't answer, I said, "I know it's hard, but he needs to see you."

He said, "I don't know where we got all twisted. I do love him."

"He needs to hear that from you."

"I don't know if I can do it."

"Come see him. Tell him you love him."

Silence.

I said, "I'll put Jimmy on the phone now." And called down the hall, "Jimmy, your dad's on the phone."

I listened to Jimmy say, "Hi, Dad," and heard Buddy say, "How are ya', Jim." And hung up the extension.

Later I asked Jimmy how the talk with his dad went.

Jimmy told me: "Oh, you know. The same. Said he might come out."

"That's all?"

It took three weeks and numerous phone calls from various family members in Texas to convince Buddy to see his son, but Buddy finally did come out, with Ophelia, on the same weekend Stasey was visiting.

I thought Jimmy just wanted see his dad, but what he wanted was to see us together. He invited all of us to go to Stephen's, his favorite restaurant downtown. He made the reservations himself: "Mitchell. Party of six."

We sat around the table with no trace of jealousy, no resentment, no heartache of a "failed marriage." All that evaporated. All those years of tears, of wanting his mother, his father, his step-mother, his step-father, to let go of any illusion of separation and to come together, even once, with love, were realized in that moment. I didn't understand, until that night, how much it means to children of divorced and remarried parents for those parents to let go of the past and simply share an evening.

We studied the wine list, discussed every item on the menu, "Oo'd" and "Aa'd" when the dinners arrived. We tasted each other's food. We laughed with ease, froze in silence when Jimmy coughed so hard he had to leave the table.

"You want me to come with you, Bro?" Stasey asked.

Jimmy nodded, holding a white napkin to his ruddy face.

In the boys' absence from the table, and in the silence that followed, we let in the sadness of seeing our healthy son assist our dying son with so much tenderness.

Frank broke the silence. "Being together like this must mean a lot to Jimmy."

"Except for that cough, he seems okay," Buddy said.

"He's pulling it all together for tonight," I said.

"Jimmy asked Stasey to a party after dinner," Ophelia said. "If he's so sick, how can he have that much energy?"

"I don't know, either," I said. "That's how AIDS is."

Frank said, "He's been looking forward to your visit. It means that much to him."

"He doesn't want to be sick while you're here," I said.

Ophelia said, "From what you told Buddy on the phone, we expected him to be much worse."

How could I explain the day-to-day deterioration Frank and I observed over the months? The good days? The bad days? The way his body seemed to be wasting away?

Frank offered: "After dinner, why don't you both come back to the house for coffee? We'll fill you in on the details while the boys are at the party. I'll show you my underwater slide show. We can talk."

Jimmy and Stasey returned to the table. I scanned Jimmy's face for any sign of disorientation. There was none. Our sons were whispering to each other like co-conspirators.

"What time's the party?" I asked.

"Whenever we get there," Jimmy winked.

I'll always remember the satisfied look on Jimmy's face as he and Stasey waved goodbye at the door on their way out to the party. All four parents settled into easy chairs in the living room, drinking coffee, preparing to watch a home slide show. Together.

August 26, two days before Jimmy died

We had rearranged the dining room, moved the long table against the wall, lined the chairs up next to each other, creating an open space in the center with seating around the perimeter of the room for the family and visitors who were expected. Jimmy lay in bed in a coma.

All those chairs, and Matt and Bobby sat on the floor in

the carpeted hallway landing overlooking the dining room. An empty dining room, except for Buddy, who sat staring vacantly out the picture window. Matt and Bobby were wrapped in each other's arms, comforting each other in their sadness over losing yet another friend. They were lovers, used to touching each other's bodies. I doubt that Buddy had ever seen two men embrace as Matt and Bobby were, naturally and without shame.

Buddy had chosen a chair in the middle of the row with empty chairs on either side of him. He was quiet, nothing but sadness on his face. I stood against the wall wondering what Buddy thought about Matt and Bobby's open show of affection.

Matt unfolded from Bobby's arms, moved toward Buddy, sat in the chair next to him. Matt said: "Jimmy and I have been friends for a long time. He's talked about you a lot."

Buddy remained silent. I couldn't tell if I saw hope in his eyes or fear about what Matt would say next.

Matt continued: "I know his relationship with you has been painful over the years. Like my relationship with my father. All Jimmy wants is for you to accept him for who he is."

It took great courage for Matt to speak to Jimmy's father like this. Matt — small framed, wiry, with dark, intelligent eyes — lived in St. Louis when Jimmy did, returned to Albuquerque shortly after Jimmy moved back. Not only to be close to Jimmy who was dying, but to be close to his own parents. If Matt had been in Jimmy's shoes, he would have liked someone to talk to his father like he was talking to Buddy.

"I know Jimmy loves you," Matt said. "And I know he'd

want you to know how much it means to him that you're here."

Matt placed a comforting hand on Buddy's knee.

I expected Buddy to pull away, but he didn't. His shoulders sagged. His head dropped. And for the first time ever I saw him cry. He wept sad, open tears that spoke paragraphs of years of a misunderstood relationship. In the space of love shared, the confusion the straight father of a gay son feels all melted away, washed in tears of sadness.

Matt slipped his arm around Buddy's shoulder, hugged him gently, then returned to Bobby's arms.

Buddy wiped his eyes, rose from the chair, walked down the hall toward Jimmy's room.

Kandi told me what happened next:

"Buddy came through the door. He'd been crying. He stood looking at Jimmy in the coma. Suddenly, without any warning, Jimmy sat straight up, opened his eyes a moment, looked right at Buddy and said, 'I know you love me, Dad!'"

Breaking Through Denial

Getting Into the System

Wednesday, March 22nd, 1989

I asked Jimmy, "Is it all right if I stay for the interview?" We were in his apartment waiting for the case manager to arrive.

"I don't care," he replied. "It's up to you."

This interview would establish his eligibility for state medical assistance.

"I'd rather not do this at all," he said.

The doorbell rang. I answered it. The woman at the door introduced herself as Vicky. I searched her eyes, wondering what I would find.

She and I sat on the sofa, Jimmy across the room at his desk. He turned the chair to face us as Vicky took out her forms and began asking questions in a soft, quiet voice. What I was hearing, hopefully, was compassion.

"Do you own any property?"

"No," Jimmy answered quietly.

It sounded like regret to me.

"Any stocks? CDs? Life insurance policies?"

"No."

"Do you own a car?"

"Yes, a 1974 Volkswagen Superbeetle. The body needs a little work, but it runs good."

As Vicky asked her questions, writing Jimmy's answers on the forms, I realized how few material possessions my son owned. But he wasn't poor, just young. Just getting started with his life. The fact that he could truthfully answer "No" to the financial questions meant he would be eligible for a number of programs, thank God. Frank and I would not have to sell our home to pay Jimmy's medical bills.

Vicky read from the form on her clipboard, "Are you able to prepare your own meals?"

"Of course I am!" Jimmy answered quickly.

He was lying. I remembered all the times I'd asked him what he'd eaten and he said he'd picked something up at a drive-in window.

She read, "Describe a typical meal you might prepare."

"Oh, I don't know. An omelette. Toast. You know."

I remembered going with him to buy his groceries and how we selected foods. I'd put a dozen eggs in the basket, saying: "They'll be a good protein source and easy to fix."

"I don't want eggs," he'd say replacing the eggs on the shelf. "They'll just go bad."

"With what frequency do you prepare your own meals," Vicky was asking.

"Most of the time," he said.

I knew he slept through breakfast. He was lucky to get one meal eaten before his shift at the restaurant.

"Are you able to get through a meal?"

"What do you mean?"

"Are you too tired to finish a meal? Not as hungry as you thought you were? Perhaps at times there's nausea?"

"Maybe," he said, looking down at the papers on his desk. "Once in awhile, I guess."

I remembered fixing him meals at our house, how he'd have to stop eating to go to the bathroom. From the kitchen I'd hear him throwing up.

"How's your energy at work?" she asked, gently.

He straightened the papers on his desk, wiped dust off the stapler, stared out the window before he spoke. "Last week I had to lie down on some boxes in the back between waiting my tables."

He peeled off a strip of Scotch tape, folded it back on itself until it was a tiny square. "I guess I have been pretty tired lately." He tossed the tape into the nearby waste basket.

I remembered when he told me about coming home from work empty-handed after he'd miscounted someone's change and got stiffed for a twenty-dollar bill. He had to make it up out of his own pocket. It left him with almost nothing to show for a full night's work.

"Do you think you could work part-time?" Vicky asked. She wasn't reading from the form anymore, but looking at him with soft eyes.

"I'm already considered a part-time worker. I barely make enough to pay the rent now. I wish I felt like working *more*. Not less."

It was the first time I'd heard him admit how hard it was for him to work anymore. It made my chest ache. He was 25 years old and would probably never be able to work again.

Vicky continued: "You know, Jim, none of this aid will be available if you continue working. It takes about six weeks to process all this paperwork. We can cancel it at any time though. You might feel better and be able to return to work."

He shook his head. His eyes darted to mine. "Fine," he sighed. "That's fine."

Hide The Guns

Sometime in April

Jimmy was tired after the doctor's visit, went home to take a nap, came over for dinner that night. He ate slowly, didn't say much except that he was tired, and that he wanted to sleep over. I made up the sofa bed in the guest room, kissed him good night on the cheek, and joined Frank in the living room to watch television.

A while later, Frank's phone rang. I picked it up. It was Jimmy calling from the guest room using my phone line.

"Well, hello," I laughed. "What did you do? Climb out the window? Aren't you just down the hall?"

Jimmy wasn't laughing: "I need help! Please. Come here!"

I took off down the hall, not having any idea what this was about, wondering, *Why doesn't he just walk out to see me?* Afraid he wasn't able to walk.

He was lying flat in the bed, eyes wide, fists gripping the sheet. He looked terrified.

"Jimmy, what is it?" I asked. "What's wrong?"

"I need you to hide the guns. Tell Frank to lock them up. Someplace I can't get at them."

I tried to hold him, but he shook me away.

"I'm scared. Scared about what's going to happen."

I sat on the edge of the bed. As close to him as I could. He didn't move over.

"If I'm gonna die, I want to die right now."

"Honey, I know you're…"

"I'm not afraid of dying, Mom," he said, looking at me for the first time. "I don't want to kill myself, but I don't want to suffer, either." He looked away, pleading: "Please, God, don't let me suffer. Take me now. I want to die *right now*."

"I don't want you to die, Son."

"I don't want to be covered in lesions like Bruce was."

"I know, Honey. It's scary."

Jimmy had showed me the spot on the bottom of his foot that morning before his visit to the doctor. He had pulled off his sock, pointed to it, rubbed it and said, "I think that could be KS."

KS was short for Kaposi's sarcoma, a skin cancer rarely seen before AIDS. The Center for Disease Control in Atlanta used Kaposi's sarcoma as one of the criteria for an official AIDS diagnosis.

"Does it hurt?" I asked about the tiny, purplish spot on the ball of his foot, just below his middle toe.

"No, but it's hard. And it looks like the ones I saw on Bruce."

"Honey, it could just be a little bruise," I said. "Let's wait and ask the doctor."

The doctor had said: "We'll set you up for an appointment with a dermatologist for a punch biopsy. So we'll know for sure."

"Will it hurt?" I heard Jimmy asking.

Their voices sounded very far away.

I knew I had to get out of that room before Jimmy saw me crying.

But I was too late. In the middle of his talk about details of the biopsy, Jimmy glanced at me. As soon as he saw the fear on my face, he started to cry too. He waved his hand at me, said, "Mom, would you please wait outside!"

"I'm sorry. I'm going," I said as I darted out the door, ashamed at my loss of control. A nurse saw me crying and offered me the privacy of her office.

All that had happened this morning, and now my son wanted to die.

"And I don't want to be in that terrible pain Tim was in before he died," Jimmy was saying. He was stretched out rigid on the sofa bed. "Mom, it's the *pain* I'm afraid of. The closer Tim got to death, Mom, the more his family blamed his friends."

"Honey, you have a right to feel afraid. I'm scared too. I can understand how you would want to kill yourself," I said, not knowing how I could watch him suffer.

"I wish God would take me here and now," he said, his eyes piercing the ceiling. "Please, God. I don't want to suffer. Take me now! Please ! ! !"

I had never seen anyone in such in-the-moment, full-of-energy fear. The fear made him believe he really could pray himself dead.

Then the idea that anyone could die just for the asking struck me as bizarre. I felt my chest and throat tighten. I knew if I opened my mouth, instead of the scream I was feeling, what would come out would be a laugh.

I had to stop looking at him. I had to look down and away. Yet I couldn't let him walk through these terrible feelings all alone. "Can I pray with you?" I heard myself asking.

"Yes. Yes. *Please*," he answered, squinching his eyes shut tight.

I placed my hands over his clenched fists, took a deep breath. Closed my eyes and prayed: "Dear God. We place ourselves in your hands. We need your help right *now*. Only you know what the future holds. Take Jimmy's fear and transform it to love. We ask right now, in this moment, to let us feel your love and compassion. Please give us peace. Amen."

Jimmy rolled towards me, drew his knees to his chest and cried. I draped my body over his, breathed with him, stroked his beautiful auburn hair, kissed his tears, and held him.

I held him while he cried, longed to tell him this was only a nightmare. That soon he would sleep. And when he woke up in the morning everything would be all right.

I longed to, but I couldn't. I wouldn't lie to him. This disease was not going away. It was here, and we had to learn how to live with it. Moment by moment. For as long as we had.

Scarlett pushed her nose between us, whimpered softly, slathered her tongue over his face licking the tears away. He grabbed the thick fur on her neck, hugged her tightly.

"I'll tell Frank to hide the guns," I said.

"No, I'm not going to kill myself, Mom. I don't think I ever really wanted to."

"We can do this, Jimmy. We can walk through this. I promise."

The Chapel
Friday, May 26th

Friday afternoon of Memorial Day weekend, Jimmy had an earache so painful he lay in bed writhing, cupping his hand to his ear, begging for relief. "Besides the pain," he moaned, "and the ringing, every sound echoes. My own voice is like a roar."

We tried eardrops, Tylenol, peroxide, a heating pad. I'd even gotten a bottle of homeopathic earache remedy. The label said it was formulated especially for babies. Because of what AIDS does to the immune system, baby remedies seem to work best, with the fewest side effects. But even that didn't help.

My sister claims that when she was a child, Grandmother cured her earache by covering her ear with a warm fried egg. I was desperate to break the strain. I said, jokingly, "We could try a fried egg."

Jimmy answered: "What are you talking about!? What am I supposed to do? Eat it?!"

"Of course not, you lay it on your ear." I laughed.

"I'm hurting!" he said, without the slightest trace of humor on his face.

How could I joke when he was in such obvious pain?

Because you feel powerless, said a voice in my head.

The doorbell rang.

"Kenny!" I said. "What a surprise!"

"Hi, Bobbie," he said and hugged me.

Kenny relaxed into a hug so well, hugging him was like hugging a teddy bear who hugged gently back.

"How's Jimmy?"

I put my arm around Kenny's waist and walked with him toward the back of the house. "He's having that terrible earache again."

Kenny peeked his head around the bedroom door.

Jimmy said, "Kenny! I thought you were in Denver."

"I'm on my way, but I wanted to stop and see you. Bobbie said your ear is giving you a bad time again."

"It's worse this time," Jimmy said, carefully holding his hand to his ear, barely touching it.

"I'm sorry, Sugar. Maybe these will help." Kenny opened a wrinkled white bakery sack he'd brought with him, pulled out a cookie. "Double chocolate chip. I saved you one! They always make me feel better."

Jimmy rolled his eyes at Kenny and said, "I don't think that'll do it."

"I love you, Jimmy," Kenny said. "I wish there was something I could do to help."

I left them alone, Kenny sitting on the edge of Jimmy's bed, crying between his soft words, holding Jimmy's hand.

When he came out, he blew his nose, and said: "I hate seeing him in so much pain, Bobbie. I feel, just, so helpless to do anything."

"I know. Nothing seems to help. I think we'll be taking him to the hospital. I'm glad you came by."

I delayed calling the Clinic. By now, I knew from many

other phone calls what they would say: "Put those drops in his ear. Give him two Tylenol." And I'd answer: "We tried that hours ago and it's just as bad."

They'd ask, "Does he have a fever?"

I'd answer, "Low-grade."

And they would say, "There's nothing we can do unless his temp is at least one hundred and one."

"Fine," I'd say. "Thanks a lot!" And I'd hang up.

Jimmy said: "I can't stand this anymore, Mom. You'd better call the doctor. Maybe he can prescribe something that'll help. Something stronger."

I knew he had to be reaching his threshold of pain. He never asked me to call the doctor. That was usually my idea, to prod him into getting something checked. By now, though, I realized just how little the doctors could do. When I would call, they'd say, "Bring him right in." But without an appointment, we'd sit in the waiting room of the Clinic for at least three long hours.

"Let's take your temperature again," I said, putting my hand on his forehead. "You know they'll ask."

Jimmy reached for the thermometer himself, shook it down like a pro, and stuck it under his tongue checking the time on his bedside clock. After three minutes he took it out, read it and said, "Ninety-nine and... maybe a half."

His normal temperature was ninety-nine. The extra half degree would not cause the doctors concern. I felt like we were off on another futile attempt to find relief, until I heard Jimmy say, "Mom. Please call."

I talked to the nurse, then gave the doctor the rundown on the phone: "Severe pain for the past five hours. Tylenol hasn't helped. Neither have the drops or anything else. Could you prescribe something for the pain? Something strong?"

"You'll have to bring him in and let me take a look."

We did.

Jimmy moaned and pulled back when the doctor touched his ear.

"What could be causing this kind of pain?" I asked.

"We can't be sure. If it's some kind of virus or bacteria, the antibiotics he's already taking should help. In the meantime…" The doctor wrote a prescription for Percocet. "This should control the pain."

As we walked out of his office, I handed Jimmy the car keys, and said: "You might be more comfortable waiting in the car. I'll get the prescription filled."

"Try to hurry."

"I will. But you know it depends on the line at the pharmacy."

I hurried down the hall past the gift shop, past the elevators, past the glass doors to the administration offices, all the while thinking: *I don't want him to have to take a narcotic for the pain. I want his earache to go away like it used to when he was a little boy, when I'd hold him, rock him while he cried, soothe him until the pain disappeared.*

I knew this new pain required a controlled substance, and maybe even that wouldn't be strong enough. Percocet would only mask the pain, not cure its cause. But the pain. We must deal with the pain.

Then, there it was, across the hall from the chapel: the pharmacy.

Ahead of me at the pharmacy window, in line, waiting, I counted eleven people shifting restlessly from foot to foot. I claimed my place, checked the time, wondered how long the wait would be, worried if Jimmy was all right in the car, tried to calm myself down when the fear came pouring back in:

This drug won't cure anything! How much worse will he get? How much more can he stand? How many more trips to this window will it take? I hate having to be here! I hate hospitals! I hate waiting in lines!

"Next."

My turn! Finally.

I handed the window-worker the prescription, Jimmy's Medicaid card and his University Hospital Indigent Status Card. The combination meant he would not be responsible for payment as long as it went through that pharmacy. The clerk didn't look at me or say anything. She took the paperwork, disappeared behind the rows of stacked shelves. A polite smile would've made such a difference.

I wanted to lash out, to scream, *Don't you* care *what's happening?!*

I felt like I was losing it. If I kept going, I'd cause a ruckus, get carted off by security, and not get Jimmy's pain pills.

Angels. Help me. Please.

I heard a calming voice whisper: *We are with you. Breathe.*

I wanted desperately to just cry.

But no, not here. Not among these strangers. Not so far from home.

I wondered if any of the other people around me wanted to cry. Or to scream. I looked at the man in line behind me. His face betrayed nothing.

"Sign here."

The window-worker shoved a paper under the Plexiglas

divider designed to protect her from us. It was only after I signed the paper and pushed it back through the cut-out slot that she handed me the white paper bag, the receipt stapled to the top.

As I passed through the pharmacy door, I glanced across the hall, saw an open door someone had forgotten to close. It was the chapel door. I peeked in. No one was there.

The oak pews looked smooth and warm in the low-level incandescent light, a stark contrast to the fluorescents in the hall. Behind the altar hung a simple painting of the white dove of peace. I thought maybe I could sit for just a minute. And breathe.

I tiptoed down the short aisle to the front pew, sat on a bench that felt surprisingly cool beneath me, took the first deep breath I'd taken in days. I closed my eyes and prayed:

Dear God. We're doing everything we know to do and it's not enough. We need your help. I need your help. Jimmy is in your hands. Hold him gently. Give me strength to face today. Help me learn how to let go.

I tried to imagine how letting go of Jimmy would feel. I couldn't. I didn't want to. Not now. Not yet. There was too much to do. I remembered the bag of pills in my lap. Jimmy's pills. I quickly got up and walked out.

There'll be time, later, for rest.

Memorial Day Weekend

By Saturday morning, Jimmy's temperature had reached 101 degrees. He was vomiting every half hour and had a terrible headache that overshadowed the pain in his ear. The Clinic was closed for the holiday weekend. Frank and I had to take him to the Emergency Room.

We found out "fever, headache and vomiting" was low priority on the emergency triage list. We waited and watched and eavesdropped on a gunshot victim, a business executive with a broken ankle from sliding into third, a smashed hand from a dropped car engine, a burned arm from a barbecue fire, all being treated ahead of Jimmy.

Jimmy lay for hours on an old gurney, on a hard, cracked, vinyl matress covered by a too-small fitted sheet, the sheet starched, stiff and scratchy. When I asked for a pillow, the orderly said curtly, "We're all out of pillows."

Occasionally, a nurse would scurry into Jimmy's enclosure, take his blood pressure, his temperature, write something on the chart and quickly move on.

Frank left to go back to the house to meet Griff, who was driving up from Midland to pick up Scarlett's weaned puppies.

Frank was gone 2 hours and 45 minutes. He returned to

the hospital surprised we were still in the Emergency Room.

"Do you have any idea how much longer it'll be before he's seen by a doctor?" Frank asked the nurse.

"They're all busy with emergencies. As soon as it slows down, one will be here."

"Damn, if we knew we were going to be waiting this long we would have kept him home."

"In his own bed," I said. "At least he'd be in familiar surroundings."

"And have quiet," Frank added.

I hated the Emergency Room. Hated the smells. Hated the way they treated him as if he wasn't really sick.

"It's probably just the flu," I heard the nurse mutter to another white coat on the other side of the privacy curtain.

It's not the goddamned flu! I wanted to scream out. *He has AIDS!*

God, how I wished it was the flu.

Ten and a half hours passed on that gurney in the Emergency Room before Jimmy was finally admitted to a room on the fifth floor. An IV was started to balance his electrolytes and offset his dehydration. A battery of tests were ordered to determine the cause of the fever and vomiting. One of the tests was a lumbar puncture. Frank went home to take care of the animals while I stayed with Jimmy to be with him through the invasive procedure.

As Jimmy signed the release giving his permission for the LP, he told the doctor: "You can do it, but please don't make me wait. The more time I have to think about it, the more scared I'll get."

The doctor said he would get the LP kit and proceed immediately.

The doctor was gone about ten minutes. He came back with the kit, opened the sterile package, told Jimmy, "Take off your underwear and open the back of your gown. And roll away from me into a fetal position."

Jimmy did as he was told.

The doctor swabbed Jimmy's lower back with Betadine to clean it, set up the drain tube and flask to retrieve the spinal fluid, got out the needle. I felt sick when I saw the diameter of the needle and was glad Jimmy couldn't see it. "Lie very still," he said. "Don't move a muscle."

Just then the doctor's beeper went off.

"I'll be right back," he said and hurried out of the room, leaving Jimmy lying on his side, bare bottomed.

"But I said I don't want to wait," Jimmy called out, but the doctor was already out the door.

We waited. And waited. Jimmy said: "He promised he'd do it right away. I can't believe I have to lie here like this."

Twenty-eight minutes later the doctor rushed back into the room. He put on a mask and gloves, grabbed the needle, and without so much as an apology for leaving Jimmy like he did, he began probing Jimmy's spine.

"Ow!" Jimmy yelled. "That hurts!"

"Don't move," the doctor shot back, withdrawing the needle and probing again.

"Ow!"

"Pull your knees closer to your chest."

"Ouch!" Jimmy cried out.

"Be still!" He pulled out the needle and again dug it into the space between two of Jimmy's vertebrae. "If you'd just relax," he said, "it'd go in easier," as if it was Jimmy's fault he couldn't find the right spot or get the needle in successfully.

I had to turn my back, force myself to stare out the window, grind my jaws, clench my fists, keep my mouth shut while my mind screamed, *Just get it over with and get the hell out of here!*

Finally, the doctor got the needle in the correct place, and Jimmy's spinal fluid began dripping slowly into the little glass tube. He put the stopper on the tube and left the room warning, "Oh, yeah, don't stand up for a few hours. And if you get a headache, have a nurse give you a Tylenol."

I hadn't said anything to stop what was happening. Now it was too late. It was done. I stuffed the feelings I had about the doctor and turned my attention to Jimmy. But I swore, by God, I was never going to keep my mouth shut again.

"I'm so sorry, Jimmy." I pulled the sheet and blanket back over his body, tucked him in, gave him a sip of water.

"It's over with now, Mom. It's over."

"Is there anything I can get you?"

"I think I just want to go to sleep. Why don't you go on home. It's late."

"Are you sure?"

"I'm really tired."

"Okay, Honey. I'll see you in the morning, after church."

When I got to the hospital after the Sunday service, the neurologist assigned to Jimmy's case was on one side of Jimmy's bed, Frank on the other. Frank said, "Dr. Ron is just beginning the neurological exam."

Jimmy's eyes met mine. I couldn't tell how he was feeling. I asked the doctor, "Is there any word yet on what's happening?"

Dr. Ron answered: "There's no way to tell yet. The results of the lumbar puncture were not conclusive."

"Not conclusive?!" I shouted. "It took that doctor five tries with that foot-long needle last night."

Frank said, "You're telling us that was for nothing?!"

Dr. Ron turned to Jimmy, and said softly: "I'm sorry you had to go through that. It must have been terribly painful for you."

Jimmy said, "That's okay, Ron. It's over with now."

That was all it took for me.

"I'm sorry I raised my voice," I said. "I know it wasn't your fault. It's just so damned frustrating."

"I understand," Dr. Ron said gently. "Sometimes anger is the only emotion safe enough to feel."

I fought back the tears that surfaced to wash away the anger, then let the tears silently fall. Frank and I stepped back and let the doctor continue the exam.

Dr. Ron asked Jimmy, "What is your name?"

"Jim E. Mitchell."

"And what's today's date?"

"Sunday."

"Do you know the date?"

"I'm pretty sure it's Sunday."

"No, the *date*, Jim."

"The twenty-seventh?"

"That's good, Jim. That's real close." Dr. Ron made a note in the chart, then held up a pencil. "What's this I'm holding in my hand?"

"Sure, it's a... a... "

"Take your time, Jim. What's it called?"

"I ca... I don't.... What was that again?"

"Could you tell me what you do with this?" Dr. Ron asked and continued to hold the pencil in front of him.

Silence from Jimmy. His eyes were closing like he was falling asleep.

"When's your birthday, Jim?"

Jimmy answered with a nursery rhyme, "Twinkle, twinkle little star."

Dr. Ron leaned in toward Jimmy and asked, louder, "Jim, when's your birthday?"

"I remember you," Jimmy answered, eyes big as if just waking up. "You're Ron. You're beautiful." Jimmy smiled, then closed his eyes again.

"Thank you, Jim. Do you… Jim, look at me. Open your eyes, Jim."

Dr. Ron lifted Jimmy's left eyelid, shined his pocket flashlight directly into Jimmy's eye. The pupil did not shrink from the light.

"What's happening?" I asked.

"Is it a coma?" Frank said. "What?"

Dr. Ron glanced nervously at us, then back to Jimmy. "Let's just let him sleep for now. See how he's feeling when he comes around."

"Jimmy. Jimmy, it's Mom." I held his face in my hands. "Can you hear me?? Honey, wake up!"

Frank put his arms around my shoulders, stood me up and held me. "The doctor said we should let him sleep now."

"Why doesn't he wake up?"

No one would say.

Frank and I spent Sunday afternoon taking turns talking to him, trying to break through the curtain that separated him from us. Letting him know we were there. Repeating:

"Everything that can be done is being done, Jimmy. We love you."

We would tell him what the nurses were doing when they changed his IV bag, when they took his temperature, and we told him to expect a squeeze around his upper arm when they were about to check his blood pressure.

Still he didn't move. No motion from the bed except for his shallow, raspy breathing. No flicker of eyelids. No twitching of nose or mouth. No movement of any kind. His temperature climbed slowly, so we sponged his forehead and arms.

Sunday evening the problem with his temperature became serious. It would be normal one minute, and the next it would spike to 105. We spread dozens of wet washcloths over his body during the spikes, trying to keep him cooled down. Frank and I took turns changing out the washcloths for cold ones as soon as they got hot.

Around midnight, Frank convinced me to go home for a few hours. He would sit with Jimmy during the night and I would take over in the morning. Frank promised to call me if Jimmy took a turn for the worse. I left the hospital exhausted, hoping the phone wouldn't ring during the night.

Frank told me, when I relieved him the next morning, that as the hours dragged slowly by, he became very sleepy, but knew he had to stay awake and keep the washcloths wet. If Jimmy's temperature rose to some critical point it would cause irreparable brain damage. He kept a supply of clean washcloths lined up on the counter, pulled the chair closer so he could watch Jimmy from between the sink and the bed. He kept up a steady stream of banter hoping the sound of his voice would help bring Jimmy back. "We love you, Jimmy," he told him. "We're right here with you. Please wake up."

Jimmy couldn't swallow while he was in the sleep and mucus formed in his throat. He sounded like he was in danger of strangling. Frank asked the night nurse why there was no suction installed in his room. She said a suction machine could be brought in and put at the head of the bed.

"Then get one in here!" Frank said, angry that a suction wand wasn't plugged into the wall outlet, that one hadn't been ordered by even one of the myriad of doctors who had wandered in and out during the past thirty-six hours.

Instead of a suction wand that plugged into the wall, a noisy suction machine was brought in. The nurse showed Frank how to use it. A long, thin tube stretched from a plastic bottle mounted on the front of the machine to Jimmy's mouth. The end of the tube had holes in it. He swept the tube all around the inside of Jimmy's lips, his mouth, over his tongue, his gums, into his throat, sucking the mucus down into the bottle, clearing a passageway for him to breathe.

Frank and I spent the next two and a half days taking turns fighting to keep him breathing and to keep the fever at bay. We weren't ready to lose him yet. Not like this. Not in the hospital. Not strangling on mucus and burning with fever. Not while in some mysterious sleep.

Dr. Ron stopped in more frequently than his regular rounds required. Tuesday he brought with him the head of the Neurological Department at the University, a much older man in a baggy, wrinkled suit, lines in his goateed face.

"It is not a coma," he said in a thick German accent. "It's a meningitis. Do not give up hope. He *will* wake up." And walked out of the room.

Dr. Ron held back. "You can trust him," he nodded. "He's the best." And smiled the first encouraging smile I had seen from him since Jimmy fell asleep. "Why don't you take a break. Go home for a while. We'll call you if there's a change."

I said, "We don't want him to wake up with strangers around him. Or worse yet, with no one at all."

How could I go home? There lay my son. Not moving. In a sleep from which none of us was able to wake him.

Heat radiated from his still body. I filled a pan with cold water, dipped the washcloth in, squeezed out the excess water, wiped down his burning face, his neck, his arms, his hands, his legs, his feet. And started over again.

Within seconds the cloth was hot, requiring redipping in the basin of water, wringing and rewiping, over and over.

I asked what antibiotic he was being given.

I heard: "There are so many we can't just prescribe one indiscriminately. We have to know exactly what's causing the infection…." *(Maybe they know, they just aren't telling me)* "Fever itself is the most effective weapon the body has to fight infection."

"If it doesn't kill him first," I said.

"All we can do is wait."

We did.

Next to Jimmy's bed.

In a room filled with the sweet aroma of Stargazer lilies and the clatter of the suction machine.

The lilies. From Rob. Huge, beautiful pinks and reds bursting color and fragrance out of their six-pointed stars.

I wished Jimmy knew Rob had brought them, arranged them in crystal vases, filled every available surface in the tiny room with flowers.

The card tucked into the Stargazer lilies read:

You deserve the best.
I love you.
Rob.

I never understood their relationship. How quickly Jimmy forgave Rob for breaking his heart. I remember standing in the kitchen a few years ago and Jimmy coming over to the house. In tears. I held him while he cried. "It's over," he said. "He doesn't love me anymore." I didn't ask questions, just held him in his pain. It took me years to piece together the real story.

Jimmy told me: "Rob got mad. He said some things." Rob told me: "I'm honest with my feelings. I got angry and showed it." At 20 years old, Jimmy assumed that rage equaled rejection forever. You must not love me if you're mad. Rob just saw himself as expressing his feelings, not: *Get out of my life I never want to see you again.* It wasn't even close to that in Rob's eyes. But that's how Jimmy took it. Jimmy was working at the bank in Albuquerque then. Rob would pass up his turn in line, wait for Jimmy's teller window, and Rob would ask: "What's the deal? Why won't you call me back?" Jimmy never did explain. Jimmy took the job with TWA and moved to St. Louis. They ran into each other at the airport one day. Jimmy acted warm and close like nothing had ever happened. They were friends again after that, but not lovers. Rob figured it was just one of those things.

Rob and I rarely crossed trails in the hospital, which was good, because there was still a part of me that blamed him for hurting Jimmy. But there were the flowers, the cards, the phone calls: "Bobbie? Rob. How's Jim?"

"No change. Thanks for calling again."

Rob was charming and handsome, closer to my age than to Jimmy's. He was always traveling to exotic faraway places, places Jimmy would have loved to visit. Rob would bring back trinkets and treasures, display them in the river valley adobe home he'd redesigned and remodeled himself. He built central halls and soaring lofts, and filled them with expensive ornaments, hand-carved furniture, and fancy antique vases. Rob would let Jimmy housesit while he was away.

I struggled to let go of my judgements that Rob did not think my son sophisticated enough for him. I asked my angels for help and heard: *None of that matters now. Put aside the blame and look for the love.*

"Is there anything I can do?" he would ask me. I finally got up the nerve to suggest: "If Jimmy pulls through this, you might take him somewhere. I don't mean getting on an airplane. Maybe just to Taos or Santa Fe. It'd mean so much to him if you'd ask."

I waited, phone in hand, through the silence on the other end. "I... I don't know," he said. "I'll give it some thought."

As far as I know, Rob never mentioned a weekend trip to Jimmy. Yet Rob was the first one Jimmy called when he was readmitted to the hospital, the first one I called when Jimmy fell into his sleep. I got him on his mobile phone.

"I'm at a construction site," he said, "inspecting a concrete pour. Thanks for letting me know."

And Rob came by, within hours, with another armload of lilies. One of many friends who visited Jimmy that weekend. At one point, I counted eleven friends lined up outside in the hall. Mike, one of Jimmy's old roommates, brought his CD player and a Sarah Vaughn disc. It was a big step for Mike to walk through those hospital doors and confront his own fear. He said, "Jimmy loves Sarah Vaughn." With the music softly playing, Sarah's voice as sweet as the flowers around Jimmy's bed, Mike sat watching Jimmy sleep.

When Mike got up to leave empty-handed, Frank asked him: "You're leaving your CD player here? Aren't you afraid it might disappear?"

"It doesn't matter," Mike said. "Jimmy needs music."

Petey phoned, said: "I want to come see him. But I can't. I just can't." I could tell he'd been drinking.

I said: "Jimmy's very sick, Petey. I don't know if he's going to make it. This might be your only chance to see him."

"I can't, Bobbie. I'm sorry, I can't."

I was angry. I said: "You're denying yourself something you're going to regret for the rest of your life. Do whatever you have to do to be here."

He started crying. "Bruce is dying. Andrew. And now Jimmy. It's too much. It seems like all I can do is drink."

"Get your butt to a meeting and get up here!"

I had very little sympathy then for people who said they couldn't do it. I do now. Now I understand.

On the afternoon of the third day of his sleep Jimmy began to awaken. His body started to move hours before his eyes opened. He scratched at his nose, moaned softly. His speech hadn't returned, but when we asked him, "Are you thirsty?" he nodded and opened his lips. We put the straw in his mouth and he sipped and swallowed, all this with his eyes closed. He pulled slowly at the end of his mustache and fussed with the sheet, until finally, by late Wednesday, I could write in my datebook: *He's back!*

When Jimmy woke from the sleep he brought some new friends with him.

"Look at those little men, Mom," he said, pointing to the ceiling. "Look what they're doing up there!"

"I can't see them, Honey." I didn't care that he was seeing things I couldn't see as long as he was back from his sleep.

He giggled, listening to voices I couldn't hear, said to someone who wasn't there, "Stop teasing me!" and to me, "They're hiding the pencil again."

"What pencil?"

He grabbed at something in midair. "This one. Right here." There was nothing there.

"What do the men look like?" I asked.

"They have funny-looking wigs and long white robes."

"How many of them are there?"

"Three, I think. They keep hiding. See? They come out from behind that ceiling tile."

I looked where he pointed, strained to see what he was seeing, tried to understand.

"I can't believe you don't see them too, Mom," he said, giggling and grabbing at the invisible pencil hanging in midair.

I told him: "I believe you *are* seeing something and I know it's real to you. You know I love you and wouldn't lie to you, but I don't see them, Jimmy."

Gradually, over the next few hours, what started out as playful little men took on a darker demeanor. He described them now as three bald men wearing black hats and black coats. They hid in the balloons Kandi brought him, peered at him from behind the bouquet of gladiolus. The IV in his arm became a deadly snake. Black flies only he could see swarmed at him, penetrated his skin. He writhed from side to side, ducked to avoid being bitten. He grabbed the IV tubing, tried to pull it out of his arm, desperate to be rid of the snake. He was afraid to close his eyes. He yelled: "One of them has a gun! They want to kill me!" and tried to get up out of bed. His fear made him as strong as three men. Frank and Linda and Kandi's husband Tom were in the room. We could barely hold him down. He kept shouting: "I've got to get out of here! Help me!"

There was no time to put on his slippers, no time to grab the robe and get it on him. All we could do was follow along and see that he didn't hurt himself. We raced to keep up with him as he took off down the hall. I steadied him with one arm, pushed his IV pole with the other. Linda kept his hospital gown held together as best she could.

He kept looking behind him to see if the men in black hats were following. And into every room, searching for a safe place to hide. He ducked into the first empty room he came to and went straight to the phone, called 911 before I could stop him.

I took the phone out of his hand as gently as I could before he actually talked to anyone. Told him: "Aunt Linda and I are here, Honey. We won't let anyone kill you."

"You don't understand, Mom. They're after me! There isn't anything you can do to stop them!"

Nothing I could say would convince him he was safe. And really he wasn't safe, even with all of us fighting alongside him. What he was seeing was more real to him than I was, or Linda, or Frank or Dik or Kandi or Ophelia or Cathy or Petey or Peter or Mother or Pat or Libby or Rob or the doctors or the nurses or all his friends who made a steady stream in and out of his room. Jimmy's world was a world of sheer terror. And he faced that world alone.

Jimmy continued his flight down the hall, dragging us along too. We rounded the corner past the nurses' station. They looked up from writing their notes, followed us with their eyes.

"Erase my name off that!" Jimmy shouted, pointing to the large board posted on the wall at the end of the hallway, listing every patient's name and room number.

The nurses shrugged as if things like this happened every day. I felt like I was in a movie.

Jimmy pulled me and Linda into a room where a young man lay propped up in bed, his face partially hidden by an oxygen mask. He had a tube in his chest with a machine draining his lungs. I recognized him from the Persons With AIDS group he and Jimmy attended. I knew his mother from our Significant Other Group.

"I need to hide!" Jimmy blurted out. "They're trying to get me!"

The man's muffled voice answered: "Sure." He pointed. "Hide in there."

The three of us crowded into the tiny hospital closet, catching our breaths in the dark. We crouched there for no more than two or three seconds when I got an uncontrollable urge to laugh. But before I could, Jimmy abruptly opened the door and dragged us out of there, Linda struggling to keep his gown closed, me pushing the IV pole along. On the way out of the room I thanked the man in the bed for letting us use his closet.

He answered, "Anytime."

Out in the hall, two maintenance men stood on a ladder with their heads above the ceiling tiles. It was like the image Jimmy had described in his hallucinations. I said, "Jimmy, those are real men fixing something in the ceiling."

"I know that, Mom." He sounded insulted that I'd made a connection between what he was seeing in his mind and what we were seeing out in the hall.

I felt confused and at a loss as to what it all meant. Were the men in black coats the virus that was trying to kill him?

Or did Jimmy need to condense the fears of a lifetime into a few terror-filled hours? Was it something his angels had arranged to help him let go of his body and all the fear associated with having a body?

I don't know. But I do know we had to help him live through that fear. We couldn't let him die, we wouldn't let him die — that week of Memorial Day.

Big Guns

After Jimmy awoke from his sleep, family members took shifts sitting with him trying to reassure him, trying to keep him from hurting himself. We couldn't risk turning our backs on him even for a moment for fear he would rip out his IVs, or try to jump out a window.

We had him moved to a "safe room" across from the nurses' station, with an extra-strength window to keep him from crashing through it, a glass panel in the door so he could be watched. For three days we pleaded with the doctors for something to calm him down.

Hospital protocol to get a tranquilizer prescribed required, first, an examination by a psychologist, then, if findings warranted, a visit by the supervising psychiatrist who was the only one allowed to prescribe tranquilizers.

After we plowed through the red tape and got the psychiatrist in to see Jimmy, after the psychiatrist wrote the prescription, after the pharmacy delivered the Ativan, after the nurse administered it, it worked like a miracle *within forty-five minutes!* Finally his body rested, even though his mind and his eyes still saw terrible things we did not. But at least we could relax a little. We no longer had to hold him down.

The attending physician called me and Frank into the hall. "Something came back in the spinal fluid culture. It's just a trace, but since nothing else has shown up, we have to assume it's what's causing the meningitis."

I held Frank's hand tight, and waited.

"It's a cryptococcal fungus. You and I have it in our digestive tracts. Our normal immune system keeps it under control."

"Why is it in his spinal fluid?"

"That's the problem. It doesn't belong there."

"Can anything be done about it?"

"There has been some success in treating cryptococcus with Amphotericin-B. It's so powerful an antibiotic we call it the 'Big Guns'."

"What kind of side-effects does it have?" By then I knew every medication had side-effects.

"Over time, there could be reduced kidney function, possibly some liver damage as those organs try to flush it out."

"Isn't that dangerous?"

"If either the kidneys or the liver shut down, yes."

"We don't want Jimmy hooked up to machines for the rest of his life," Frank said.

I said, "I want my son out of the hospital."

The doctor looked me straight in the eyes, gave me the facts: "If cryptococcal fungus is left to grow unchecked, it's fatal. It might take a few months, but Jim will surely die without the Amphotericin. I've seen it before. It's a painful, frightening death. Fever and vomiting. Horrible headaches. And more hallucinations. Worse than what we've experienced over the last few days."

The doctor continued: "If he tolerates the test dosage

we'll begin the infusions immediately. We'll give premeds to reduce the allergic reactions."

"Like what?"

"Benedryl for rash. Tylenol for chills and fever. And Demerol."

"Infusions. What do you mean 'infusions'?"

"Amphotericin is administered IV. A four-hour drip once a day for six weeks."

"Six more weeks in the hospital?"

"We can arrange for home care."

"And that would take care of it?"

"We'd need to continue a maintenance dosage after that. Once a week, depending on how his kidneys react."

"For how long?"

"For the rest of his life. We need your permission to start the treatment."

"My permission?" I asked.

"We don't believe Jim is mentally competent at this time to make this decision himself."

All week long various doctors had accused me of interfering in their treatment of Jimmy. They'd threatened to move him to another hospital if I wasn't happy with his care there. When I got angry at one of the doctors, she accused me of needing psychiatric help. But now that they wanted to treat him with something that could kill him, the doctors didn't want the responsibility. I was suddenly being asked to decide what was best. I knew if the Amphotericin was to work, it had to be because Jimmy made the decision himself.

"We'll go in," I said. "You explain to Jimmy what you just told me, in as simple terms as you can. I'll be there. I'll watch him. I'll know if he understands."

I took a breath. Frank nodded reassuringly. As we followed the doctor into the room, I silently asked our angels: *Please help us here. If ever your presence was needed, it's now.*

When Jimmy saw me and Frank walk into the room with the doctor, I knew from Jimmy's eyes he knew something important was about to happen. He was alert and scared over what he was about to hear.

The doctor did a good job condensing what he'd just told me and Frank. My eyes stayed riveted on Jimmy's eyes. He listened attentively, his eyes clearer than I'd seen in days.

When the doctor finished, I reiterated, "There's a possibility this drug will not save your life."

"But, Mother, I'll *die* if I don't take the medicine!"

"Yes, Honey. But the medicine could kill you too."

"But I'm not ready to die!" he pleaded, his eyes both fierce and desperate.

A window of comprehension happened in that moment. He understood. He wanted to live.

He wanted to risk the "Big Guns."

God Rage

I left the hospital later that evening, exhausted after endless battles with doctors for Jimmy's dignity, and hours of pleading with the nurses for compassionate attention. Frank was already home taking care of the animals. At least I wouldn't have to deal with hungry animals, dirty bird cages and dog shit. I was looking forward to sitting with him in the swing on the patio, sharing a glass of wine and private talk.

I stepped into the elevator, sighed with relief that it was empty. After the smooth drop, I emerged to walk the long corridor toward the exit. I passed a white-coated student doctor, our shoes on the tiled floor echoing the length of the hall. I stepped around a janitor pushing a wide dustmop, the waxing machine waiting nearby.

I bumped through the heavy glass doors of the ER entrance into the nearly-empty parking lot. Pools of yellow light littered the pavement. I spotted my car standing alone and waiting in the far end of the lot, an oasis in the dreary surroundings. Keys in hand, I checked over my shoulder to make sure no one was following. Forced myself not to run. If someone was hiding I didn't want to show panic. I listened for footsteps behind me, looked through the car window into the backseat before unlocking the door. I slipped into the driver's seat and quickly relocked the doors. Only then did I breathe a sigh of relief. Jimmy needed me. I couldn't let anything happen.

I drove past the hospital's abandoned security gate and into the empty, monotonous street. This was the only driving I'd done in days, this route from home to hospital and hospital to home.

Time did one of those slow blinks and I realized miles had passed with no recollection of landmarks along the way. No turns. No signs. No stoplights. I'd even missed the Veterans' Memorial Park I always watched for, the flowerbed, the flag waving in the spotlight.

My mind churned with tortuous memories. *Has he been in the hospital only five days?* I recalled the prayers I'd practiced and delivered non-stop like a desperate litany.

My knuckles grew white from gripping the steering wheel. My spine stiffened so straight my hair brushed the roof of the car. My lungs sucked in, filling my body with breath. *How much worse can this get?*

I screamed: "GOD DAMN YOU GOD! I TURN MY SON OVER TO YOU AND *THIS* IS WHAT YOU LET HAPPEN?? YOU SONOFABITCH! WHAT KIND OF A GOD ARE YOU!?

I screamed harder and louder than I'd screamed in years, my face flushed and alive. My shoulders grew broad and wide, full of power. I felt my body charge with raw energy.

I staggered into the house, slammed the door behind me making noise with every step. I threw my purse on the kitchen table, kicked off my shoes, sent them flying.

Frank met me in the kitchen from the back of the house.

"What is it? Is Jim all right?"

"I could kill something!" I yelled, pounding my head against the refrigerator door. "I turn Jimmy over to God and this is what happens?? This *nightmare*?!"

My knees buckled. Frank grabbed my elbows before I hit the floor, wrapped his arms around me, held me tight.

"Let it out, Bobbie. You have a right to be angry. We all do. Go ahead, let it out."

I buried my face in his chest. Banged my fists against his back. Over and over.

"Frank," I cried. "We're losing him. A piece at a time."

Seizure

I got off the elevator at 5-West, turned down the hall, saw people gathered outside his room. So many people were there in the hall, I thought more of his friends had come to visit. But as I tried to identify who they were, I noticed the white coats, the stethoscopes hanging around their necks. I ran down the hall, pushed through them. Heard murmurs behind me. The word "seizure."

Frank stood on one side of him, Sean, Jimmy's friend from St. Louis, on the other, each holding one of Jimmy's hands. A translucent green oxygen mask covered Jimmy's flushed face. His eyes darted, bewildered, confused.

"What happened?" I asked Frank, knowing he would tell me the truth. My eyes searched Jimmy's face again, Jimmy's body, looking for signs of injury... trauma.... *There's blood on the pillowcase. His mouth is swollen!*

"He had a seizure," Frank was saying. "Right after you left."

"What's wrong with his mouth?" I raised my finger to touch Jimmy's cheek, but stopped just short, afraid I might hurt him.

"It came on so fast we didn't have time to get the tongue

depressor in. He bit the inside of his mouth. And his lip. Other than that, he's all right."

Jimmy opened his mouth to show me. *Good,* I thought. *He understands what we're saying.* But the oxygen mask was there and I couldn't see very clearly.

I kissed his forehead, felt the coolness of his skin with my lips, ran my fingers through his damp hair. "How are you doing, Sweetheart?"

Frank said, "We were telling him what happened when you came in."

"You're just fine," Sean was telling Jimmy. "We're right here with you."

Jimmy shrugged with his eyes, still groggy.

"The doctors say it'll take him awhile to come out of it," Frank was telling me. "They say he'll be tired. And he won't have a memory of what happened."

I should have stayed. I should have been there. I should not have gone to dinner with Florence.

Then I was glad I hadn't been there. That I hadn't seen the seizure. I would've been helpless to do anything but watch. I saw who had been there: Frank and Sean. Sean had come all the way from St. Louis just to see Jimmy. Jimmy had been surrounded by love.

The next morning I was alone in the room with Jimmy. He sat up in bed, reached toward his right foot, said: "Mom! Look!" His foot, tucked under the hospital sheet, was shaking back and forth, up and down.

I watched the tremor spread under the sheet to his knee. To his hips. Then his entire body seized rigid. His jaws clamped tight. His teeth crammed shut. There was no time to reach for the tongue depressor wrapped thick with tape.

The nurse had hung it near his pillow on the bed rail, ready for anyone to grab in an instant and quickly put in his mouth. She'd said: "Place it between his tongue and the roof of his mouth. It'll prevent him from biting a hole in his tongue. Once the jaws clamp shut, don't try to open his mouth," the nurse had instructed. "If you get your finger between his teeth, you could be bitten horribly. You have to be fast to get the depressor in his mouth. It will happen that suddenly."

I seemed to be hypnotized by the involuntary movements his body was taking. My mind said: *This is a seizure! Quick, grab the depressor!* But all I could do was watch his body arch and stretch out, convulse from side to side.

His legs had straightened out and were quivering. His left arm curled up and his hand went into a fist. His right arm stretched out open, reaching up, shaking. His head leaned back, his neck very, very rigid. His eyes were open but had widened, unfocused, and he was looking up over his head. I could see the ring of the iris but not the pupil, white with a little bit of green showing under the upper lid. The upper lid was about two-thirds open, about a third of the way closed, not blinking. His jaw was set, his muscles tight. I was afraid he was going to bite his tongue in two.

Someone had come in and was holding his right hand, trying to pull it down. I said: "No, no, let it go. Don't try to restrain him. Let him reach. We just want to keep him from falling out of the bed." I had my hand on his left shoulder and I knew he wasn't trying to get out. All he was going to do was shake. We had the side rails wrapped and taped with sheets, but he was shaking so violently the padding didn't seem like enough.

The nurse had said the actual seizure would only last a few seconds and I prayed for the seconds to pass without his injuring himself: *Please, God, help him through this.*

In the midst of the tortuous-looking seizure, I heard reassuring whispers say: *It'll pass. Soon. It'll pass.*

I watched, amazed at the transformation in his body. His neck relaxed, his fists unclenched, his body softened and melted into the bed. His eyes closed mercifully. His breathing returned to almost normal. I rearranged the sheets, smoothed them out, straightened out his pillows, searched his body for bruises. I looked in his relaxed mouth for blood. Tried to convince myself he wasn't hurt. How could he not be feeling pain?

I was limp, exhausted. My body felt racked. Like I had been caught in the middle of nowhere with nothing to hang on to but a single, spindly tree while the storm raged all around me. I wondered how long I could hang on without getting sucked away.

No wonder the nurses checked his seizure medication to keep the seizure activity controlled as much as possible. He couldn't be held or comforted during seizures, just watched and protected from personal injury. When he came out of it, he had no recollection of the experience.

"How are you feeling?" I asked him.

"I'm real tired."

"Want a drink of water?"

He took a sip, worked his jaw back and forth.

"Is your mouth okay?"

"It's a little sore."

"Do you remember anything?"

"I remember seeing my foot take off by itself. That was...

what?" He looked at the clock. "Two hours ago?!"

He really was okay. I was the one who needed comforting. I was the one who needed to be held during his seizures. To keep me from losing myself in the hopelessness of seeing my child's body go through torment, and not being able to do one damn thing about it.

Jimmy was home from the hospital.

His friend Peter came by the house to visit him every chance he got. Peter was an accountant. His mind was quick. He frequently talked at the same time as the person he was talking to was talking. I used to think he was interrupting, or not listening, but I quickly learned he was taking in everything the person was saying. He was just saving time, getting more information out by talking while the other person was talking. I could follow along with him, but then I'd start laughing, get lost sorting out who was saying what. I had to both think about what I was saying and process what Peter was saying. Peter was a real challenge to my slow Texas talk.

Peter moved back to Albuquerque from Denver to be near is family when he tested HIV-positive too. They had agreed long-distance (Peter in Denver, Jimmy in St. Louis) to each be tested: "I will if you will," they'd said to each other over the phone.

"I'm scared."

"Me too."

"Let's do it."

"This week?"

"Deal."

"Call me."

"Don't tell anyone."

Peter's father was a doctor, his mother a nurse, and the medical procedures surrounding Jimmy were familiar to him. He was very helpful, wasn't scared at the sight of blood. He'd volunteer to empty and rinse the urinal. He'd hold the emesis basin while Jimmy vomited, then wipe Jimmy's forehead with a cold, wet cloth and wash the basin out.

One night Peter and Steve-O came over to be with Jimmy while Frank and I took a break and went out to dinner. They brought a bag of tacos to share with Jimmy and Laura, his nurse.

"Now you two go out and have a nice time and don't worry about a thing. We'll be fine," Peter said, at the same time we were saying: "Here's the number of the restaurant. Give a call if anything happens."

When Frank and I returned, we heard laughter and animated talk filtering down the hall from Jimmy's room. "Thank God everything's all right," Frank said. We walked straight back to tell him we were home.

Taco wrappers and Coke cups still littered the bedroom. Peter and Laura were sitting on the bed pointing at snapshots, Steve-O standing beside them snickering.

"Hi, Mom! Hi, Frank!" Jimmy smiled from the bed. "How was dinner?"

"Delicious," Frank said.

"It's a beautiful night out," I said. "There's a full moon."

I wouldn't tell him about asking Frank to pull over and just hold me while I cried.

I said, "Looks like you've been having a good time."

"Peter and I were telling Laura about that Halloween party

we went to in Denver. We were looking at the pictures when you walked in."

Laura said: "I just love this one of Steve-O in his Navy lieutenant's uniform."

"What a party," Peter said. "Seems everyone was there."

"Look at this one," Jim said, held one out for me to see.

I laughed and shook my head. "Those black fishnet stockings really top off your outfit, Jimmy."

"Here's another one," Steve-O said. "That's the year you won first place in the contest at Mama Mia's restaurant."

"Ms. Truck Stop USA," Peter smiled.

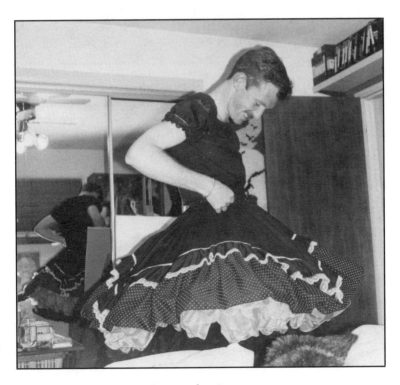

Jimmy dressing up

Jimmy as Ms. Truck Stop USA

"Please. Don't remind me," Jimmy said, shaking his head. "That was the year Ronny was supposed to do my makeup. He was driving from Kenny's in El Paso, stopped to see a friend in 'Cruces. They got so stoned that Ronny was in Arizona before he realized he was headed the wrong way."

God, how I loved hearing him laugh out loud, seeing him visit with his friends, looking at pictures, treating the nurse like she was one of the boys. He was an hour into his Ampho treatment. The premeds had worked. This was when he had the least pain, the most energy and the best appetite.

I walked around to the side of the bed. "You look so good. Can I have a hug?" I slid my arm under his neck to hold him close for just a second.

He cried out, "My neck!"

His body arched, stretched, and went rigid. I felt ripped inside. Grief flooded my entire body.

Peter and Laura grabbed pillows, stuffed them between Jimmy's head and the headboard, between his shoulders and the side rails.

I heard my voice screaming: "My baby. My baby. No!"

I let the wall support me. Let my legs go out from under me. Let my body slide toward the floor.

Peter turned away from Jimmy, swept me up in his arms. "Got to take care of Mama," I heard as he lifted me up, carried me out of the room to my bed and laid me down. "You rest here for a while," Peter said. "I'm going back in with him. Frank will take care of you now."

Frank nodded, sat on the bed next to me and held my hand and let me cry.

"I can't stand seeing him that way," I said. "If I hadn't tried to hug him, he wouldn't be going through that. It's all my fault. All I wanted to do was hold him."

"It's not your fault, Bobbie. The doctor said there'll be more seizures. But go ahead and cry," Frank soothed. "I know it's scary."

"God, yes! He's in so much pain."

"He only looks like he's in pain. Remember?"

"What?" I blew the tears out of my nose.

"He'll have no memory of it. It's like an electrical shock to the brain that effects the memory while it's happening. All the synapses are firing at once. He'll have no recollection of the seizure. There's no way he can be in pain."

"Are you sure?"

"Yes," Frank said. "I'm Sure."

Peter stuck his head in the door. "Jimmy's fine now. He's sleeping," he said softly. "You guys okay?"

"Yes, we are. Thank you," Frank said. "We appreciate what you've done, Peter."

"He'd do the same for me. You two try to get some rest before Laura goes home. I'll be back tomorrow."

Taking Control

How Much Time

Late June

He had been home from the hospital less than a week. A registered nurse would arrive at ten p.m. to do the nightly infusion. They'd start by administering premeds to reduce the side effects of the Amphotericin, wait an hour for those drugs to take effect, then infuse the Ampho through an IV drip that ran into a Hickman infusion catheter surgically implanted in Jimmy's upper chest and threaded through the subclavian vein into his neck. Because of the danger of anaphylactic shock, Jimmy's vital signs required close monitoring throughout the six-hour ordeal. If all went well, the nurse would slip quietly out the door around four the next morning.

We were told Jimmy should consume large quantities of water to counteract the side effects of the powerful drug. The water would help flush his kidneys and liver. So Frank bought a distiller, knowing it would provide the purest, sweetest-tasting drinking water available. But Jimmy said the water tasted metallic, like the drug. He wouldn't eat or drink anything he didn't like.

I'd slip into Jimmy's room each morning, exchange his untouched glass of water for a fresh one from the distiller, take a moment to watch him sleep, to watch him breathe, to verify for myself he'd survived the night's treatment.

Sometimes he'd say through half-closed lids, "That water you left last night tastes terrible."

I'd answer, "I brought a fresh glass, Honey. It'll taste better." I'd bend the flexible straw towards him knowing he probably wouldn't touch it. And if he did take a sip now and then, how could he take in enough water when he was awake only a few hours a day?

On this particular morning he got out of bed around noon, and still in his bathrobe, came into the kitchen, with Scarlett following close behind. I was setting up the distiller to restart the eight-hour process. Jimmy sat at the kitchen table. Scarlett nuzzled his thigh through his robe, rested her head on his knee.

"Here you go, Honey," I said, placing a fresh glass in front of him.

He picked it up, looked through its crystal clearness, and sighed, "More water, huh?" Resigned, he sipped it.

Good, I thought. *He didn't make a face at the taste. Maybe this will be one of his good days.*

Between sips, he stroked Scarlett's head.

"I checked my pillow this morning," he said. "It's covered with my hair. It's that way every day when I get up."

"The normal person loses between 80 and 90 hairs a day. Count them," I laughed. "If there's not more than that, it's not too many."

"Mom, seriously, I wonder whether this medicine's going to work." He took another sip. "And how much time I really have."

I poured a gallon of water into the distiller, set the empty jug under the drip spout and turned the switch on. The fan and motor made a humming sound in the quiet kitchen.

Finished with the distiller, I went through the motions of preparing his breakfast.

He was no longer hungry when he first woke up. His appetite, meager as it was, wouldn't arrive until later in the afternoon, after his system had about twelve hours to recover from the previous night's infusion.

I put water on to boil for his oatmeal, remembering how he used to love a big bowl of Life cereal mixed with Honey-Nut Cherrios drenched in half-and-half, fresh raspberries dumped on top. Now all he ate was oatmeal. He couldn't digest the seeds from the berries, and milk contributed to the constipation that plagued him.

"Mom?"

I placed a single slice of bread in the toaster and pushed the lever down. Before he was sick, he used to eat at least three pieces of toast slathered with real butter and piled high with raspberry preserves. He really liked his raspberries. Now he'd be lucky to finish half a piece of dry toast.

"Mom, did you hear me? I said I wonder how much time I really have." He seemed calm, even serene, with Scarlett's head resting in his lap.

I stared at the toaster, asked my angels: *Help me to say what you want me to say. Help me to say what he needs to hear.*

I knelt next to him, ran my hand down Scarlett's back. I looked up, met Jimmy's eyes. He really wanted an answer.

I heard myself say, "Rather than asking how much time you have, why not think about what you want to do with the time you do have?"

Saying those words seemed the most natural thing to do at that moment. But... *My God! I can't believe we're talking about this!*

His eyes went from questioning to hopeful, and he said, "Like what's really important to me?"

We were quiet then. I returned to stirring the oatmeal and saw the faces of Jimmy's friends scroll across my mind.

He said, "My friends, I guess."

"That's funny. I was just thinking the same thing."

I set the bowl of oatmeal and the toast on the table, put my other hand on his hand that he had resting on his crossed knees. I looked at his face, saw the night's growth of red beard stubble, looked into his gentle, green eyes.

"Honey," I said. "Nobody knows how much time any of us has left." I forced myself to hold back the tears that welled behind my eyes. Tears would betray my fear that we didn't have much time at all.

Jimmy looked at me a thoughtful, private moment. Then he nodded and smiled that tiny, crooked smile that was easy to miss if you weren't looking for it.

"Thanks for the oatmeal, Mom," he said as he picked up the spoon. "I think I am kind of hungry after all."

Stasey

They were brothers. Stasey was born first. He came out fighting, blue eyes squinched tight, fists doubled, determined to be born. Jimmy arrived eleven months later, a pound lighter, an inch shorter, with green eyes, ears that stuck out, and a gentle love for life.

Stasey, 16 months, and Jimmy, 5 months

Jimmy and Stasey

How different, everyone said, could two brothers be?

They fought, they wrestled, they teased. They hated each other and they loved each other. They knew that no matter how the world changed around them, they would always be brothers.

Stasey wanted to know everything I could tell him about HIV and what we could expect. He and his wife Mary lived in a tiny southwest Texas oil town, and it wasn't easy for them to learn the truth about AIDS, much less discuss it freely with anyone except each other. Jimmy and Mary and Stasey grew up together, went to the same high school. And now Mary encouraged and supported Stasey's and Jimmy's developing adult relationship.

So we had long talks on the telephone. About his relationship with Jimmy now, and how much they cared for each other. About the pain of watching Jimmy suffer and the fear of losing his brother. About "opportunistic infections," and AZT, and T-4 blood cell counts, and "wasting syndrome," and time. Stasey would ask me, "Mama, do you think I should fly out there to see him?"

"He'll get worse before he dies, Stasey. We have no way of knowing how much time he has left."

Stasey came every chance he got (with Mary's support and encouragement). Every long weekend. Every vacation. He didn't care what he and Jimmy did. What was important was that they were together. Whatever Jimmy wanted to do, Stasey wanted to do it too. Stasey embraced Jimmy's world, a world so different from his own.

For instance, Jimmy said during one of Stasey's visits: "Ronny and The Honeybees are playing at the El Rey tonight. Want to go?"

Stasey and I looked at each other. "Sure," Stasey said. "Who are The Honeybees?"

"You know. You met Ronny the last time you were here. He came over to cut my hair."

"Oh, yeah. But what are The Honeybees?"

"It's a group he performs with. Come on, it'll be fun."

I said, "I'm game if you are, Stasey."

"Can I wear my cowboy hat?"

Jimmy laughed, "You're so good-looking, you can wear anything you want. They'll love it."

"Stasey, The Honeybees are three female impersonators."

"Aw, Mom, I wanted to surprise him," Jimmy teased.

When we arrived at the theater it was packed. The Honeybees performed *"Stop in the Name of Love"* as Diana Ross and the Supremes. They were beautiful. And talented. And everybody laughed and hooted and whistled and had a great time. Stasey had never seen anything like it. What might have been an oddity before Jimmy's illness was now good, clean fun. Seeing the performance through his dying brother's eyes let him watch without any judgement whatsoever.

Jimmy said, "Everyone will be down at *The Sōc'* after this. Tonight's country music night."

Jimmy loved to dance and Stasey loved country music.

"Sounds fun to me," Stasey agreed. "What's *The Sōc'?*"

"It's a gay bar," Jimmy said easily.

"Oh. One of those," Stasey answered uneasily.

"No, it's not like that, Stasey. This is a private club. You don't even have to buy a drink."

"Do you have to be gay?" I asked for Stasey.

"They don't care who you go to bed with. Much less who you dance with. You'll see," Jimmy winked at Stasey.

Jimmy signed us in as his guests. And as we threaded our way through the crowd, he stopped frequently to introduce us.

"This is my mother."

"Hello."

"And my brother, Stasey."

"Glad to meet ya'll!" Stasey said in his Texas drawl, and shook hands over and over.

As we worked our way near the dance floor, four young men stood up from the best table in the house, offered it to us. A member bringing his mother and his straight brother was probably not a usual occurrence. We were being treated like royalty.

Almost immediately, a man with a handle-bar mustache wearing a peach colored shirt and a bolo tie asked Jimmy to dance. We watched. Neither Stasey nor I had ever seen so many people of the same gender dancing with each other. Here at *The Sōc'* it didn't seem strange at all. Everyone was relaxed, comfortably laughing.

Jimmy returned to the table smiling, face flushed from dancing. "What do you say, Stasey? Want to dance the next one?"

"Who with?" Stasey asked, and looked around, a little uncomfortably.

"With me. Who else?"

"Sure," Stasey shrugged. "But I don't know how to follow."

"Good," Jimmy said. "I don't know how to lead!"

And with that, they sashayed onto the dance floor, falling into an easy Texas two-step. This was Jimmy's moment. We were in his world where he could be who he was without fear and without judgement. His mother watching, witnessing, and his brother participating, enjoying. I wouldn't have believed how much fun I could have watching my two sons dance together.

I heard a voice ask, "You're Jimmy's mother, aren't you?"

I turned to see a handsome man with full, rosy cheeks, wearing a white cowboy hat, standing next to the table.

"Yes, I am," I smiled proudly. "And Stasey's, too. That's Stasey dancing with Jimmy."

"Jimmy told me how excited he was about Stasey coming to see him. His visits mean so much. It's great you're here too. Not many parents would do this, you know."

I looked in his eyes. Seeing the pain, I nodded, understanding that his parents would probably never come here. "My name's Bobbie," I said, taking his hand.

"I know. Jimmy's talked a lot about you. My name's Bobby, too."

Instantly, I felt not only proud Jimmy had talked about me, but curious just what it was he'd said. I hoped... no, I knew from the look on Bobby's face it was good. That was enough for me.

"Would you care to dance?" Bobby asked.

"Thank you," I smiled. "I'd love to."

We joined the couples on the floor, moved in a counter-clockwise direction to George Strait's *"Deep Water"* rhythm. Bobby nodded politely as we passed Stasey and Jimmy, spun me around in a California twirl that felt so free and fun. Stasey spun Jimmy in a circle, trying to imitate Bobby's fancy move, but Stasey didn't raise his spinning arm high enough to clear Jimmy's head. They crashed, laughed, and kept on dancing. God, how I loved that night.

During the Memorial Day hospitalization, I called Stasey to report Jimmy's serious condition.

"I'll get the next plane out."

"Good. Jimmy's been asking about you. Come straight to the hospital."

"Mama?"

"Yes?"

"I want him to know how much I love him. I'd like to crawl in bed with him and hold him in my arms."

"You can do that, Son."

"But he's in the hospital. Won't there be people around?"

"There's nothing to be ashamed of. You can hold him."

"Okay, Mama. Tell Jimmy I'll be there."

I was alone with Jimmy when Stasey arrived. Jimmy scooted over and patted the bed so Stasey could climb in beside him. Stasey never took his eyes away from Jimmy's eyes. In spite of how sick Jimmy was, I saw an energy happen between them. I wanted to stay to bask in their love, but I let them have their privacy. I left the room quietly, closed the door behind me, walked down the hall to where Frank was waiting.

I was surprised when Frank handed me the camera and said, "It could be the last picture we get of them together."

I took the camera, but struggled with the question of intrusion.

"Go ahead, Bobbie," Frank urged. "They won't mind."

I asked the angels, heard them say, *It'll be all right.*

I walked back down the hall, opened the door, slipped quietly into the room. Jimmy was talking.

"Is there anything of mine you'd like to have?"

"Well, Jim, that's a real nice cowboy hat you have."

I moved against the wall without looking at either Jimmy or Stasey until I saw them through the lens.

They were lying close together, talking softly. I took a slow, deep breath, let it half-way out, let the flash illuminate their faces.

Thank you, angels, for this moment.

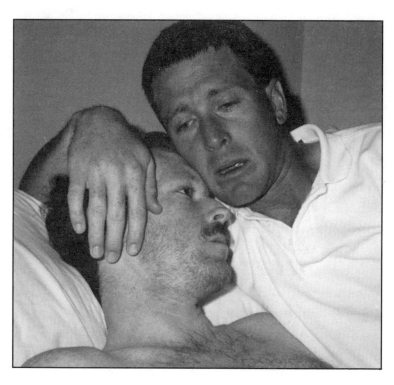

Jimmy and his brother, Stasey

Dinner For Three

Jimmy was home from the hospital. I was in his bedroom watching his favorite late afternoon soap opera with him. A commercial for a seafood restaurant came on, showing smiling waiters, plates steaming with food.

"That looks so good," he said. "I haven't had Scampi in a long time."

I thought about running out and buying the shrimp and looking up the recipe for Scampi, when he asked:

"Think we could go there tonight?"

Go there? I didn't want to face the crowds that would surely be at the restaurant on a Friday night. Didn't want to face the unpredictability of Jimmy's health. It could change so fast. It was one thing for him to get sick and throw up at home, another in public. I didn't want to leave the safety of our home. But how could I deny him?

"What time do you want to go?" I asked.

"I'm hungry now. You think you could ask Frank to come home from work a little early?"

"Sure," I said. Maybe it would be a relaxing evening out. "You start getting dressed. I'll call Frank." But I couldn't stop myself from thinking the worst.

Frank said: "It's Friday night. They don't take reservations. We don't know what will happen while we're waiting."

"I know."

"Will he have the energy to order? Then wait for the food to arrive? And when it does, to actually eat it?"

"He wants to go," I said.

"Okay, then. We'll go. Is he ready?"

"He's showering now."

Jimmy's shower, which used to take fifteen minutes, now took over an hour. He had to rest on the stool before shaving. Before brushing his teeth. And again before combing his hair. He took great pride in his appearance, but selecting his clothes, buttoning the shirt, pulling on the socks, tying the shoes left him with little energy to do the very thing he was getting dressed to do. In this case, go out to dinner. Frank came home smiling and cheerful. I knew he was hiding his fears.

We arrived at the restaurant without incident. Frank dropped us off at the door, parked the Wagoneer while Jimmy and I went inside. The lobby was packed with people. We claimed our place in line.

A girl with a clipboard and pencil asked: "Your name, please? And the number in your party?"

Frank stepped in, asked, "How long is the wait?"

"About fifteen minutes," the girl answered cheerfully.

Frank and I looked at each other. Then we both looked at Jimmy. I asked Jimmy, "Is that okay with you?"

"Sure. I'm fine, really. If I can just sit down."

The girl called out: "Sam. Party of four."

As Sam's party rose to follow, we grabbed their seats on the bench. I checked the time on my watch. If the wait wasn't too long ...

"Maybe I should take my pills now," Jimmy said. "I'm thirsty, anyway."

"On an empty stomach?" I asked, knowing he shouldn't.

"Oh, it'll be fine," he answered confidently.

"I'll get you a glass of water, then," I said.

"No, no. That's all right. I'll get it myself."

He rose before I could stop him, talked to the girl with the clipboard. She disappeared out of the lobby.

She returned a minute later with the water, handed it to Jimmy. I could see a slice of lemon floating on top.

I said: "You're right, Jimmy. I would've forgotten the lemon."

He put the pills on his tongue, washed them down with a swallow of water.

"She forgot the ice," I said. "Let me get some for you."

"No, Mom. Ice makes the pills hard to swallow."

I'd forgotten. He hadn't.

On the bench across from us, a toddler climbed all over his mom's lap. We sat quietly watching the boy. I leaned over, whispered in Jimmy's ear: "I remember when you were that age. Couldn't slow you down for anything. You were so cute." I touched his cheek. "You still are, you know."

He stared at the child. His eyes grew red and filled with tears. I could only imagine what he was thinking.

"Frank. Party of three."

"Finally."

We followed the hostess through one full dining room, up a ramp and through another full dining room, into a third room, to the only available table in the back.

"I'm feeling a little woozy," Jimmy said as soon as we were seated.

His face had paled. Beads of sweat had formed on his lip. "You need something in your stomach, Honey," I said.

I jumped up, grabbed the first waiter I saw and told him, "We need some crackers at our table. *Now.*"

The waiter brought a basket of crackers. I pushed it in front of Jimmy. He picked one up, turned the package over slowly in his hand, pulled the strip of red cellophane, slid a single cracker out, finally started nibbling it, all the while staring at the menu, closed in front of him.

Our waitress came. I opened Jimmy's menu for him and watched his expression. His face had an innocent look as if he'd never seen a menu before. It changed to concentration, then to confusion. He lifted his eyes, looked around the restaurant not quite sure where he was. I looked at Frank. Saw the concern on his face. I felt panic moving up my chest. I struggled to act normal, to give the waitress my order. I did. Then Frank ordered. Then it was Jimmy's turn and I knew he couldn't do it.

He sat staring at his right hand, flexing his fist. The waitress asked him, "And what about you, sir?"

Jimmy said, "What?" and looked at her. Then he looked at Frank. Then at me.

I wanted desperately to rescue him (or was it us?) from embarrassment. I wanted to tell the waitress to just double up on my order. *And do it fast. We have to get him home.* Instead I said, "Wasn't it the Scampi you wanted, Honey?"

Relieved, Jimmy said, "Yes." He returned his attention to his fist, stared at it, flexed it slowly again.

"Very good, sir. Would you like soup or salad with that?"

Jimmy looked up, as if surprised she was still there.

"What?" he said.

"Would you like the New England Clam Chowder or the tossed salad?"

He looked at me, asked, tentatively, "Salad?"

I nodded affirmatively, not knowing what else to do.

The waitress scribbled on her pad. "And what would you like on that salad, sir? French? Thousand Island? Blue cheese? Ranch? Or House?"

Jimmy's forehead wrinkled. His eyes narrowed as he tried to take in what she was asking. It was excruciating to watch. I wanted to order for him like I did when he was a little boy. But he wasn't a boy anymore. I had to allow him to make his own decisions even though some deadly battle of viruses was going on in his brain that impaired his ability to think and to reason and to decide such a simple thing as which dressing to put on a salad he didn't have the appetite to eat!

"Could you repeat that?" he asked the waitress.

She did, friendly and patiently, oblivious to anything being out of the ordinary.

I watched Jimmy struggle. He looked at me with *Help!* written all over his face. I said, "What do you think about Ranch, Jimmy?"

"Ranch," he said quickly, and reached for his water glass. He tried to close his right hand around it, but his fingers must have gone numb. He had to use both hands to pick it up.

He was taking a sip when the waitress asked, "Would you like baked potato, home fries, or rice pilaf, sir?"

"What?!" Water spilled down his chin, onto the front of his shirt. He didn't wipe it. Neither did I.

"Baked potato, home fries, or rice?"

This time he looked to Frank for help. Frank looked at me. I looked back to Jimmy and said, "Rice?"

He looked up at the waitress and stated emphatically, "Rice!" Then he brought the water glass up to his lips again with both hands. I watched closely, afraid he would drop it. Wanting, but not daring to help.

"And would your vegetable be broccoli? Green beans? Corn? Or okra?"

This time he pleaded with me. I answered to him, not to her, "Think you'd like broccoli?"

Jimmy nodded, "Broccoli," dropped his head and stared at the empty plate in front of him.

I was so scared I wanted to scream.

As soon as the waitress left with the orders, I touched Jimmy's forehead and said, "Honey, are you all right?"

"I'm gonna be sick," he said, barely able to keep his head up.

We'd run out of time. We had to get him out of there.

Frank pointed to the nearby emergency exit. He said: "Start moving him to that door. I'll find the manager, have him shut off the alarm."

As I helped Jimmy to his feet, I said, "That door's the shortest way out. Can you make it?"

"I'm okay. I can walk."

But when he moved he shuffled his feet, taking tiny, baby steps. In the time it took us to maneuver around the table Frank was back supporting Jimmy's other side. The manager hurried by sorting through a ring full of keys. He selected one and opened the "EMERGENCY ONLY" exit door.

We stepped outside into the heat.

"I'll get the car," Frank said. "Will you be all right here with your mother?"

Jimmy nodded, his head hanging. He rocked unsteadily

on his feet.

"I've got you," I said. "It won't be long now, Honey."

If I can get him home everything will be all right.

Frank screeched up in the Wagoneer, left the engine running, the air conditioner on "High" while he jumped out and opened the back door for us. "I told them to make the order to go. I'll run get it."

I guided Jimmy into the backseat. I slipped in next to him, shut the door behind me hoping the air-conditioning would work fast. If his temperature cooled down maybe he wouldn't get sick.

But his head rolled back. "I'm gonna throw up," he said.

I reached across him, opened the door on his side. He leaned out, and vomited and vomited and vomited into the hot parking lot. People walking by us stared. I didn't care. Jimmy was all that mattered.

I used handfuls of Kleenex to clear his nose and mouth. Forced myself to look out on the pavement to see what had come out. I couldn't believe it. How could half a saltine and a few sips of water generate so much?

Frank ran up carrying several plastic bags of food. He shut Jimmy's door, jumped in the driver's seat, and asked, "Should we take him to the ER?"

"No, let's take him home. See if his temperature goes down."

As we sped off, I asked Jimmy, "Honey, would you feel better with your head in my lap?"

He didn't respond.

I pulled him gently towards me, cradled him, stroked his face. Felt his hot skin. The air conditioning wasn't helping. I got a wet-wipe from my purse, cleansed his forehead, cheeks and mouth, talking softly to him all the time: "We're on our way home, Baby. It'll be all right."

We helped him into the house. Helped him undress and get into bed. I turned on the ceiling fan, wiped his face with a cool, wet cloth again.

"Feels good to be home," he said.

"We had quite a time, didn't we? How are you feeling?"

"I'm hungry."

"Really?"

"Yeah, I want to eat something."

"Are you sure?"

His skin was flushed, his face still swollen from the pressure to his head from vomiting.

"Why not? I'm starved."

"It's just that you were so sick. Do you remember what happened?"

"Well. We sat down to order. And that waitress kept talking and talking and talking to me. I got sick. And then we came home. Now I'm hungry."

Just twenty minutes ago we were deciding whether or not to race him to the Emergency Room. He really did seem fine now. But the virus was like that. Attack, then back off. Thank God we had brought him home. All we could do was deal with what was happening in the moment. And in that moment we were at home. Together.

"Let's eat!"

Frank brought the restaurant bags into the bedroom, and said, "Let's have a picnic!" He spread the boxes of food on Jimmy's bed.

"All right! Jimmy smiled. "I didn't know you brought it home!"

I sorted through the boxes. The food was still hot. I handed Jimmy his. "Is this what you wanted?"

"Scampi. My favorite," he answered, digging in, eating like he had never been sick, licking butter off his fingers. "Mmmm. It's great."

The three of us — Jimmy, Frank, and I — sat eating seafood dinners straight out of the containers watching Vanna turn the letters on *"Wheel of Fortune"* like the last hour had never happened.

Let's Have a Party
Late July

Jimmy came into the kitchen, freshly shaven, his hair neatly combed. Maybe this would be one of his rare good days. Maybe he wouldn't feel nauseous. Maybe he wouldn't feel like sleeping all day. Maybe he would be pain-free. Maybe his energy would last the whole day.

"Mornin', Sunshine," I said. "You're looking good." Seeing the toothbrush in his hand, I asked, "You want me to put that in the dishwasher for you?"

The nurse had suggested sterilizing the toothbrush after each brushing to help control the thrush in his mouth.

He ignored my outstretched hand. "No, I'll do it." He opened the dishwasher door. "Are these dirty?"

"I was waiting for your toothbrush to turn it on."

He dropped the toothbrush in the silverware tray and reached under the cabinet for the soap.

"That's okay, Honey. I'll do that. Go sit down."

"Fine," he sighed, and sat down at the kitchen table, in Frank's regular seat, with his back to the window, and watched me add the detergent and turn on the dishwasher.

All he had on were his yellow seersucker shorts. Coming out of his bare chest just above his right nipple, hung the six-inches or so of infusion catheter line. The hole in his skin was covered with a two-by-two square of clear plastic bandage.

That catheter was a godsend. It kept him from having to be stuck with needle after needle for medications and Ampho infusions. Blood was drawn from it regularly for tests and when he needed it, about once a week now, blood was transfused through it. The catheter was an amazing invention. But if it got infected, or if it clotted, it would have to be removed and the infection brought under control with even more antibiotics before another one could be implanted. I watched it carefully, checked it many times a day to make certain we wouldn't have to go through yet another procedure.

"How's the catheter looking this morning, Honey?" I peered closely through the plastic cover at the insert point in the skin looking for redness and swelling.

"It's fine," he said, patting it without looking down.

"I don't want that getting infected."

"Neither do I," he said, almost to himself. His legs were crossed at the knees. He swung one foot back and forth, the plastic tubing bumping against his chest.

The wound in his chest from the catheter was a constant reminder to me of the seriousness of his condition. As much as I welcomed denial, when he wasn't wearing a shirt, the tubing and valves served as a stark reminder that this man-made object would be in his body for the rest of his life. I wished he could live without it, yet having it meant less suffering and a higher quality of the time he had left.

"I've been thinking," he said. "About giving a party here at the house. For my birthday. Do you mind?"

"Of course not, Honey. I think it's a terrific idea!" I added. "How can I help?"

"I can handle it," he said.

He had forgotten about AIDS again.

He'd invited me to his parties before. They weren't just a matter of having a few friends over and throwing out some chips and dip. To him, that wouldn't be a party. Jimmy took pride in offering elegant surroundings: cloth napkins instead of paper, china instead of throw-away plates, a linen tablecloth, gourmet food he had spent most of the day preparing, easy jazz playing in the background, flowers he had lovingly arranged.

I knew he wanted to do this party right and I wanted the "finished product" to be the way he envisioned it. I didn't want to take away his fun of planning the party, but I was certain he didn't have the energy to do it. I could help make it happen.

"I'll do the work," I said. Then added, "You can supervise. We'll have fun doing it together!"

"There's nothing to it," he answered, and picked up the yellow legal pad. "I'll make up a list of who I'll call. The food. The cut flowers. And that'll be it."

"How many people are you thinking about inviting?"

He started writing: "Let's see, there's Rob. He'll want to bring Heinrich. And Dik. And Petey. John. Peter. Matt and Bobby. Steve-O. Maybe Kenny will be in town."

I smiled, "I'll call him myself. Make sure he comes. I want this to be the best birthday party you've ever had."

Jimmy frowned and continued: "And Dennis and Ed. Think that's too many?"

"No, not at all. It's a big house," I said, worrying where was he going to find the energy for such a big party. I told myself to show enthusiasm, not worry. Giving Jimmy a birthday party, maybe his last, would give me something to think about besides AIDS. "I'll invite Pat and Tom. Florence and Hannes. Libby and Don."

He said, "If I asked your friends too, Mom, the party could get out of hand."

"What's the name of that flower shop your friend, Gary, owns?"

"The Silver Petal."

"He could deliver some arrangements. And Barry from the Deli could cater it. Yeah. We could even have a waiter. Wouldn't that be neat? Everyone could just sit back and be served. Let's see, we could move the chairs back, pull the dining room table out... "

But he was getting up, walking down the hall to his bedroom. "I think I'll go lie down for a while."

I followed him down the hall to his bedroom, chattering to his back, "It could be the biggest birthday party you've ever had!"

"Smaller parties are better sometimes, Mom."

"But you have so many friends. It'll be nice to have all of them over for this birthday."

He sat on the edge of his bed, catching his breath and looking flushed. "Sure. Anything you say. Right now I want to take a nap. Okay?"

From the doorway, I watched him lie down. Watched him adjust the rented electric hospital bed, pull the sheet to his chin, close his eyes.

"Sleep tight, Honey. I'll close the door so Scarlett doesn't disturb you."

"I'd rather have the door open," he said.

I left him then, tiptoed down the hallway past his bathroom, past the kitchen where he'd told me his party plans. I went into the living room on the opposite end of the house from where he lay resting. Whatever noise I made hopefully would not disturb him. I wanted him strong for the party I was planning.

I stretched out in the recliner. Felt my temples pounding. *The party I was planning? What am I doing?*

Oh my God!

What have I just taken away from him!

Unfinished Business

Life Support

Tuesday, August 1, 1989

Jimmy was back in the hospital. It was five days before his twenty-sixth birthday. I was alone with him, in his hospital room, discussing whether we should cancel his birthday party.

"I could invite everyone to come to the house anyway, if they want to. The food and the flowers will be there. We could eat and visit awhile. Then we could come up and see you."

"Mom, I don't want to open any presents while I'm in this hospital. I'll wait until I get home to open them."

The pain was under control. Only because he hadn't had anything in his stomach since yesterday. After six weeks, the doctors had ordered the daily Ampho stopped for one week before trying a weekly maintenance dose. But Jimmy didn't get to wait the full week. On the third day without the Ampho, Jimmy was re-admitted to the hospital with severe abdominal pain, vomiting and fever.

Tests were run. As the results came back, the doctors would report possible explanations for each symptom:

"The high amylase level indicates pancreatic distress." He was in acute pain. Until the amylase level dropped, he would receive nothing by mouth.

"His liver levels are abnormal. Indicating some form of

hepatitis. Could be a reaction to the Amphotericin." Little could be done but watch the results of the liver tests.

"There is some renal malfunction. This could also be due to the Ampho." Since he was unable to urinate, he would have to be Foley catheterized or the bladder would rupture.

"The cryptococcal infection is still present, and more virulent than our last culture." Amphotericin was resumed, but at a lower dose because of liver and kidney damage.

"We'll watch his Dilantin level to try to control the seizures, which could be caused by either the cryptococcus returning or Listeria, a bacteria which showed up in one of the blood cultures. We'll start him on another antibiotic and hope...." A normal immune system has a high resistance to Listeria. Unchecked, it can cause meningitis. Which can cause seizures.

God. Please. Not another bout of meningitis.

The doctors often gave the test results in numbers, as if we knew what they meant. We learned to listen between the lines, to ask questions: "What are the side effects of the drug treatments?" "What symptoms can we expect if this drug treatment is refused?"

Jimmy told the doctors: "There's no way you're cutting on me. What good would it do? You already have me plugged into all these lines. If you operate, no telling how long it'll be before I'll feel decent again. And what do you think you'll find?"

"We don't know. But if there's a tumor, we could remove it. If the gallbladder is bad, we could take it out. You could have less pain."

"And in the meantime, there'd be an incision. Imagine if I vomited with stitches in my stomach! It'd be gruesome."

"Then there's nothing else we can do but feed you IV and try to control the pain."

If I hadn't heard with my own ears what the doctors summarized, if I hadn't asked so many questions to clarify in simple terms what they were actually saying, if I hadn't been right there with Jimmy through the entire process, I would not have believed a person could be that sick and still be coherent, even laughing on occasion, making his needs clearly known. He maintained his personality, didn't curl into a fetal position and look vacant in the eyes like I'd seen others do. He remained remarkably present in spite of what was going on inside his body.

The oncology specialist interrupted our birthday party discussion: "There are two more KS lesions on your foot, Jim. We can treat the ones we can see with radiation."

"Will the radiation hurt?" he asked her.

"Not the treatment itself. It's just like taking a picture."

"Just one picture?"

"Well, we'd do the first one while you're still in the hospital. You'd return to the Cancer Center for the other treatments every day for seven to ten days, depending on..."

"Depending on what?" he asked.

"Depending on how the skin holds up to the radiation."

"What do you mean?" His voice tightened.

"For most people, the effect of the radiation is like a minor sunburn. There'd probably be some redness. And maybe a little tenderness."

"For most people? And what about others?"

"It depends on the sensitivity of the skin. Some people develop blisters like a second degree burn. But it will heal."

"Things aren't healing on my body so easily these days,"

Jimmy said, and looked at his foot. "I wouldn't be able to walk on it, would I?"

"The radiation would reduce the size of the sarcoma," she said, trying to convince him. "It's summertime. You can go barefoot."

"But it isn't painful now. Actually, it doesn't bother me at all. Tell me again, what good would the radiation do? Will it cure the KS?"

She looked uncomfortable. She re-examined the bottom of his foot, pressing on the lesion.

Finally, I spoke: "Please be honest with him. He has a right to know."

She took a breath, looked at me, then looked back at Jimmy and said, "We haven't had much success in curing Kaposi's sarcoma. But the radiation might help prolong your life."

"My foot will be burned. It'll hurt. I won't be able to walk. I'll have to be wheel-chaired around everywhere I go."

"But it will slow down the growth of the KS," she insisted. "You'll live longer."

"Too many other things are hurting in my body. I don't want a burned foot on top of everything else."

As I watched and listened to him having this dialogue with this doctor, I kept thinking: *This isn't fair. He shouldn't be having this conversation. Why can't I wake from this nightmare? Hear some doctor, maybe this one, walk through a door and say it was all a mistake. That he doesn't really have AIDS. Or say that they've found a cure. "You'll be all better. Just take this pill."*

"It's your decision," she said, sounding disappointed. "But if I were you, I'd do anything to try and stay alive."

"You're not me. You don't have AIDS. You have no idea what I've already gone through. I don't want radiation."

She turned around and left the room quickly.

I asked Jimmy: "Was that hard for you to do? To tell a doctor no?"

"Not really. I don't want my foot burned. I just want to go home, Mom. I want this to all be over with."

"I know you do, Honey."

"I know I'm going to die. I don't want to prolong it. I don't want to feel any more pain than I already do."

I unclasped the chain to the gold cross that hung around my neck. It was the first time I'd ever taken it off. As I placed it around his neck, he said: "Mom! You're letting me have your cross?!"

He lifted his head for me to fasten the chain, laid his head back on the pillow and held the cross tenderly between his thumb and forefinger, laid his hand flat against the cross against his bare chest against his heart. Tears formed in his eyes. "It's beautiful," he said.

The cross was given to me three years ago by a woman I was assigned to in hospice just before she slipped into a coma. She was 33 years old with a husband, and two sons ages 9 and 13. She had breast cancer, didn't want to "burden" her family by dying at home. So she came into the hospital, to a room on the floor below where Jimmy was now. I held her hand while she lay in coma, told her it was all right that she let go, that she could die now. A single tear rolled out of her eye, slid down her cheek, and she stopped breathing then.

That cross meant a lot to me.

"I wouldn't want anyone else to have it but you, Jimmy."

"But Theresa gave it to you," he said, touching it again.

"And I'm giving it to you. Can't a mom give her son an early birthday present?"

He reached his arms out to give me a hug. "I'm never going to take it off."

His chart had "DNR" printed on the front in big, blue marker letters. "DO NOT RESUSCITATE" meant if he went into a cardiac arrest or for some other reason stopped breathing, they were not to call a "Code Blue" on him. But let him die, naturally.

"Jimmy," I said, "Pat and I were talking about the DNR on your chart. She said DNR doesn't cover the same things a Living Will covers. She gave me a copy of one. Want to read it?"

"Sure. I guess."

Frank and I had Living Wills executed for ourselves. Neither of us wanted to be kept alive by machines if our body was trying to die. It seemed the thing for us to do, but I never thought I'd be offering one to my son.

"What do you think, Mom?" he asked after he read it.

"It's completely your decision, Son. You have to decide for yourself what you want."

"I'm not asking you to decide for me. I want to know what you think."

It was important for him to know what I thought because I would be the one taking care of him. I did not want to speed up his death, yet I did not want him to suffer. He was afraid of the pain and I was afraid of watching him suffer and I didn't want to let my desire *not* to watch him suffer affect his decision. I asked my angels for help.

Dear angels, I prayed. *Help…me…help…him.*

I heard from my heart that I should repeat like a mirror for him what he himself had said over the past few months.

"Well, Honey, you've said you're not afraid of dying. Has that changed for you?"

"No. But I don't want to be in pain when I do."

"There are a lot of things the doctors are offering to do to you that they think will help you live longer."

"But I don't want surgery. And I don't want chemo or radiation. I don't want to lose my hair and have my skin burned. And I don't want to take drugs that will make me throw up more than I already am. Bruce told me how sick he got from the chemo and radiation for his KS. I can't take that, Mom. Bruce tried all that and died in pain anyway."

Jimmy had a sensitivity to all but one or two of the drugs he'd taken over the past few months. He had severe allergic reactions to some. Most of the time we couldn't tell if he was sick from the drugs they were giving him or from the disease itself.

"It looks like your liver and kidneys have tolerated just about all the Ampho they can," I said.

"I'm so tired of all of this," he sighed. He shook his head, read from the blank legal form in his lap: "'I do not fear death itself as much as the indignities of deterioration, dependence, and hopeless pain.'" He looked up at me, said: "Mom, I know they can keep me alive for a while. Even if I could eat, I'll get skinnier than I already am. I don't want to die looking like a skeleton."

"Jimmy, I want you to be able to live like you want to live. I'll support any decision you make."

A loud voice in my head said: *You should be talking him out of this! You'd be a better mother if you convinced him to live! At all costs! If he signs this form, he'll die!*

I took a deep breath. Tried to slow my pounding heart. I heard a quiet voice whisper a single word: *Listen.* Then: *Let-Him-Live-His-Own-Life.*

"Mom, tell Frank to go ahead and fill this out for me. I want to sign it. I want you and Dad to sign it too. And Ophelia and Frank as witnesses."

"Why don't you take some time to sit with this, Jimmy. You don't have to do this now."

"No. I know what I want, Mom. There's nothing else I want the doctors to do."

I picked up the form, kissed him on the cheek, ran my fingers through his thinning hair. "I love you so much."

"I love you too, Mom," he said. "Bring the form back up here tonight. When Dad and Ophelia come."

"We'll be here, Honey. Try to get some rest."

Frank and I picked Buddy and Ophelia up at the airport. They'd flown in from Texas for Jimmy's birthday party. We'd originally planned to have it at the house. But Jimmy was in the hospital, so in a pouring monsoon, we loaded the flowers Gary sent from the Silver Petal, the food Barry catered from the Deli, the peach and teal colored balloons. We loaded everything, including a dozen friends, into four cars, formed a caravan, hauled it all up to Jimmy's room. I set the butter-cream birthday cake with the purple orchids on top, in his lap in the hospital bed. Frank lit the candles. We all sang "Happy Birthday." His last one. We got to see his face reflect 26 candles. Got to see him surrounded by friends and flowers and balloons.

Jimmy took a bite of his birthday cake, tasted it. He had to spit it out. Any food he ate caused severe pain.

The party was over. Everyone else had gone. Buddy, Ophelia, Frank and I stayed in his room. Frank brought out the five copies of the Living Will he'd drawn up at Jimmy's request.

"Thanks for doing this for me," Jimmy said casually as he signed them.

Then Buddy signed. I signed. Frank signed. Ophelia signed. Frank handed one to each of us to keep.

"There," Jimmy said. "That's done. Make sure the doctors have one in my file."

"I'll take your copy," Frank said. "I'll watch and be certain the nurse puts it in your chart."

Just then the door opened and Petey stuck his head in. He had timed his visit to the hospital to arrive after everyone had left, he had hoped. He didn't want to be around a lot of people.

I didn't know what it was like to be Petey, to be a person proven statistacally to be "high risk" for developing AIDS. I didn't know what it was like for Petey to watch his friends, to watch his peers, his buddies get sick and die all around him. I couldn't know the terror of wondering day to day if "I would be next."

"Hey, Girlfriend," Petey said, walking into the hospital room looking like a drenched rat. His curly hair was stringy now from the rain, pulled back into a ponytail, dripping, the outline of his stocky body showing through his rain-soaked T-shirt. "Sorry I didn't make it to the party." Then seeing all of us, said, "Am I interrupting?"

Jimmy said: "Come on in. We're through here."

"I'm sorry I'm so late," Petey said, coming closer to Jimmy. "But I didn't get a ride and so I walked in the rain and... well... here." He'd been hiding a hand behind his back holding a green plastic dinosaur that looked like a cross between a Tyrannosaurus Rex and Godzilla. He thrust it out toward Jimmy. "Sorry it's not wrapped. Happy birthday, Sister."

Jimmy looked bewildered as if to say, Why are you giving this to me? But said instead: "Thanks, Petey, it's... weird."

"Well, I guess I'll be going now."

"If you wait a few minutes, we'll give you a ride home," Frank offered.

"Thanks anyway," Petey said. "The walk will do me good."

"Are you sure?" I asked. Petey's heart was raw and tender. I wanted to let him know we cared, but I didn't want to intrude on his space.

"Really. I'd rather walk," he said. "You take care, Jimmy. I'll be talking to you."

"Thanks for coming by, Sugar."

When Petey left, Jimmy told us: "It's been hard for Petey. First Andrew died. Then Bruce. And if that wasn't enough, Patrick committed suicide last week."

A silence in the room. Finally, Ophelia said, "I don't understand how you all do it."

"We cry a lot, Ophelia," I said.

"And we hold each other," Frank said. "How do you do it, Buddy?"

Buddy shook his head slowly, staring at the floor.

"There isn't AIDS where we come from," Ophelia said, answering for Buddy.

"Where's the camera?" Jimmy asked. "Frank, while you're putting my Living Will in my file, ask the nurse to come in and take a picture of the five of us. Then Frank, I want you to take Mom and Dad and Ophelia to Sadie's for some real New Mexican food." Jimmy winked. "Have some for me. Okay?"

"You betcha," Frank said. "It'll be my pleasure."

"Hey, you all better get going. The streets are going to be flooded." Jimmy's hand touched the gold cross lying around his neck. With the other hand he waved goodbye. "I love you guys," he said. "Thanks for letting me do it this way."

Letting Go

I went to bed scared. Again. Before sleep, my mind reviewed the day. Eyes wide open, I stared at the ceiling remembering his birthday party. It didn't turn out anything like I had planned. And thinking about the papers. How openly he talked about it and signed them. We all signed them, wondering, "God, what does this mean? Will he starve to death?" I hated going to bed afraid of tomorrow. Each day held terrible surprises. Nothing could be predicted or expected. Besides, we didn't want to know anymore.

Mornings my mind usually sorted itself awake. My thoughts would always find Jimmy. I'd wonder how his night had been. If he was comfortable. I scanned all the things going on in his body, questioned whether he was in pain. Was I forgetting to do something? I had learned from my work with hospice and from being with people who chose to die consciously that acceptance comes when "unfinished business" is taken care of. Not only for the person dying, but for the family who surrounds him. When there is a clear sense of completion, a peaceful, quiet death follows. Was anything left unsaid? Friends to connect with? Had he done everything he could do?

I sat on the edge of the bed the next morning knowing somehow something was different. Something changed while I was sleeping, and I thought: *Phew! So this is what it feels like. There really is such a thing as letting go.*

I breathed in the lightness. Felt the first absence of denial, the first moment without fear. This is what I'd hoped for, prayed for, didn't think possible. The struggle had vanished. I had relinquished power, surrendered to events out of my control. *Thank you God. Thank you angels.*

Then I got scared.

"He must have died!"

"What?!" Frank said, suddenly wide awake.

"Something's happened," I answered, pulling on my clothes. "I have to get to the hospital. NOW!"

"Why don't you call first? See how he is?"

"No, I have to go. I don't want to hear over the phone: 'I'm sorry to have to tell you this, but Jimmy died during the night.'"

I don't remember getting there. But I do remember standing alone in the elevator waiting for the doors to open. I remember stepping out, voices at the nurses station as I turned down his hall. I remember slowing my walk when I saw the door to his room was closed. It was never closed. I hesitated, not wanting to see inside. But I had to know. Slowly I pushed the door open.

He was sitting up in bed looking right at me.

He's alive!

Smiling. So open. No sign of fear. No pain. No struggle. Aglow with energy. It was the same room. The same IV lines. The same bed. But somehow he was different. There was more of him there than I'd ever seen.

"Wow!" he said. "That's so neat! I was just thinking about you walking through that door. The door opened and here you are!" He patted the bed next to him, the side without the IV poles. "Come here," he said.

I sat of the edge of the bed and took his hand like I always did.

"No," he said. "Don't sit. Lie down next to me." He rolled away from me onto his side. "I want us in spoons."

I had watched him stretch out on our carpeted floor with Scarlett, his front to her back, his eyes closed contentedly and a soft smile on his face, like a little boy holding the teddy bear of his dreams. I envied Scarlett because of how freely and comfortably he gave affection to her. And now without any embarrassment, like it was the most natural thing in the world, he was asking me into bed with him. I accepted his invitation in awe.

I snuggled in close to him, touched him carefully, felt the heat of his body where our bodies touched.

He said: "I can't believe the love I feel for you right this minute. I've never loved you as much as I love you right now."

I could feel my breasts against his back. I put my right arm up over his head, rested it on the pillow, pressed the front of my thighs against the back of his thighs, rested my left hand easily on his left shoulder.

We lay in silence for a while. I knew he could feel me breathing against his back. He said, "It's almost like we're lovers instead of mother and son." Then the silence filled with wonder like a moment in blessed eternity.

He turned his head around, shifted his hips enough to look at me, and said, "I want to see your face."

I shifted my position, laid my arm lightly on his abdomen,

careful not to put weight on his body, amazed he wasn't in pain.

He said, "I can't seem to look at you enough, Mom."

I felt flooded with open love. I felt *BIG!* His heart moved up through his eyes. Eyes so alive it seemed rays were coming out and filling me. The veil that separated us melted and... and... I couldn't hold the tears any longer.

I sat up on the edge of the bed with my back to him, covered my face with my hands and cried. "I'm sorry I'm crying, Jimmy. I'm sorry."

I felt the bed sag as he propped himself up on his elbow, felt his hand touch my shoulder. He said, "Mom, I don't *ever* want you to apologize for crying."

All those years I'd held back the tears, afraid to upset him or scare him. He had every right to hold back his love, to punish me for abandoning him as a child, for sending him to live with his father and his step-mother. That deep-seated resentment was always between us. All I could do was let him know I'd never leave him again. As long as he lived. I would never leave him. This was the first time I felt he'd forgiven me. The first time he let himself just love me.

I dropped my hands from my face and turned to him. He held me while I cried.

"I love you so much," he said.

The woman who cleans the room came in. Jimmy continued to hold me. We didn't move. She emptied the trash next to the IV poles.

Jimmy said to her, with his arm still around me: "This is my mother. I love her."

The woman smiled at us, broom and dustpan in hand, and took in the picture of us on the bed.

Jimmy turned his face to me, said to me, "I told her I love her, too." He turned back and said to her, "Didn't I?"

She nodded, still smiling, and quietly left us alone.

"I've been telling everyone I love them. It's like my love is coming out. All over!"

Oh my God! He must be dying! HELP! What do I do?

I pulled a Kleenex out of the box, blew my nose, choked back the fear that threatened to take me away. I heard: *Set aside the fear. There'll be time later to grieve. Be with him now. In the love.*

"I'm ready to tell you what I want at my memorial service," he said. "Write this down."

I picked up the yellow legal pad we kept by the phone. Frank had carved a hole in the pad, tied a string through it and tied a pencil to the other end of the string, so anyone visiting or answering the phone while he slept could pass on messages. The top page was full of messages. My eyes stopped on a happy face next to "*Steve-O sends his love!*" in what I recognized as Peter's handwriting.

I turned to a new page.

"I want flowers. Lots of flowers. And Mom, I don't know if you'll be able to do it, but would you write my eulogy? And I'd like you to read it, too. And I want my friends to say something about me. And I want pictures there. And show that old home movie of us on the swing in the backyard of me and Stasey when we were kids. You know the one I'm talking about, Mom. Do you think Frank could do that? Oh, and I've decided I want to be cremated after all. And my ashes up on the mountain. Tell the church to put out extra chairs. I think there'll be lots of people there...."

Elizabeth

Jimmy was replacing the receiver on the telephone by his hospital bed when I arrived at his room the next morning: "That was Elizabeth," he said. "She wants to see me. She's flying out tomorrow."

I remembered when she had first called (Was it only a month ago?) from the airport, on her way to a conference in Utah. She said she had only a few minutes between flights, that she hadn't heard from, or about, Jimmy since they were in high school together. All she knew was that he lived in Albuquerque now.

She'd looked him up in the phone book, called his listed number. The disconnect recording gave her our home number and when she called it, I had answered the phone.

She identified herself. She said: "Jimmy and I were best friends in high school. And in the youth group. I was passing through and thought I'd say hi. It's been years since we've talked."

Jimmy was asleep in his bedroom, still tired from last night's Ampho infusion. I asked the angels if it was all right to tell this young woman the truth. *Yes,* my angels whispered. *She's a friend. She wants to know.*

"Jimmy's sleeping now, Elizabeth. I'd wake him, but he needs to rest as much as he can."

"Oh?"

"He's been living with us since Memorial Day. He's sick, Elizabeth. Jimmy has AIDS."

In the moment between my last word and her next, I was afraid I'd done the wrong thing telling her.

"No! I had no idea! No one told me! I didn't know!" She sounded angry, then concerned. "I'm so glad you told me. That I called."

I started breathing again. My angels didn't lie.

She said: "I want to see him. Do you think I can see him? I'll write first if I need to. Or call. When's a good time to call?"

"Whenever you want, Elizabeth. I'll tell Jimmy we talked."

As soon as Jimmy woke, I told him about Elizabeth's call.

"My God," he said. "Elizabeth." His eyes shone brighter and wider than I'd seen in what seemed like such a long, long time. "We haven't talked or written since I graduated high school. How did she.... Why now?"

"I don't know. Maybe it's a God thing and your angels arranged it."

"She didn't know." His face showed surprise and then wonder. Then disbelief. Then pleasure. "Elizabeth... "

After that, it seemed there was a card in the mail from her nearly everyday. And when the phone rang, often it was Elizabeth calling long-distance from Texas. And now she was coming out to see him.

He was nervous. "Gosh, it's been so many years since she's seen me. I wonder what she'll think."

I watched him with his feelings, trying to imagine what this must be like for him. "She must care a lot about you, Jimmy, to fly out here to see you."

"We were best friends, Mom. Elizabeth, me and Alicia. The three of us did some of the craziest things. Those trips with the youth group. One year we took a trip to Florida. Bill and I dressed in grass hula skirts, used those coconut things for boobs. We danced for the group around the campfire at the beach. God, how we laughed. We could always find something to laugh about."

The next morning, I took my camera to the hospital knowing Elizabeth would be there. About mid-morning I went out into the hall to get a drink of water. Even though I'd never met her, never even seen her picture, I knew the girl in the blue denim shorts, red T-shirt and short summery hair cut coming towards me was Elizabeth. Her eyes were friendly and open, not afraid. Not afraid of seeing Jimmy sick.

"Elizabeth?"

"Bobbie." Her hand reached out to shake mine. She said, "I recognize you from the picture Jimmy showed me back in high school."

"My picture? He showed you *my* picture?" It took me a moment to realize what she was saying.

"Yes. He carried it in his wallet. Jimmy said he couldn't talk about you in front of Buddy and Ophelia. But he talked about you all the time with me."

I hugged her. "All that's changed," I said, hoping it would stay that way. "Ophelia was a good mother to him when I couldn't be there. I know now how much she loves Jimmy. And how much he loves her."

"He loves you too, Bobbie."

I hugged her again. "Come on in. He's really looking forward to seeing you. He's a little nervous."

"So am I."

I took her by the hand and led her to the open door of his room. I stopped at the door, let her pass by me, looked in and watched his face, his reaction. I wanted to give them their privacy, but I didn't want to miss seeing their first moment together.

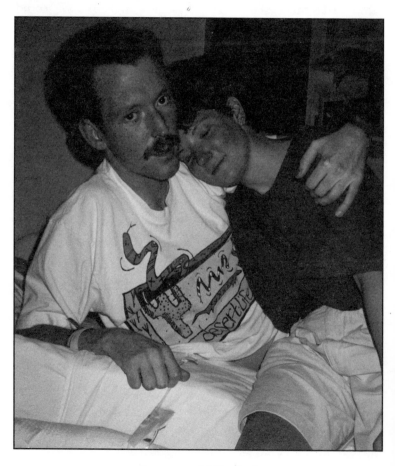

Jimmy and Elizabeth

After awhile she came out into the hall, said that Jimmy was tired and that he wanted to take a nap. "When I look at him I see so much love in his eyes." Tears welled up in her eyes. "I don't want this to be happening to him. He deserves so much more."

"You gave him a lot of love back when he was having a hard time finding it."

"Jimmy was the one who gave me the love. I could always count on him to be there for me." She turned away, wiped her tears. "How do you make it through all this?"

"I cry too, Elizabeth. Sometimes crying is all we can do."

One Month Later

Elizabeth wrote me about her flight home from Jimmy's memorial service:

My plane was delayed leaving Albuquerque by about three hours so it was night by the time I left. All the way to Dallas there was a lightning storm in the distance. It was a clear night everywhere, no bad weather around the plane, but off in the distance, I watched lightning dance in the clouds and I felt Jimmy. I kept thinking: All the energy that was Jimmy could do anything now. He could dance in the clouds if he wanted to. Out of that sick body. It was beautiful.

The Spray Bottle

Ed and I met in the hospital hall. Ed was open, talkative, full of energy. He sold real estate. He was one of the gang who made the annual Labor Day lake party, a ritual Jimmy looked forward to every year. Ed had made a get-well card for Jimmy, had it signed by all of the guys who went to the lake.

We walked together back to Jimmy's room.

"How is he today, Bobbie?" Ed asked.

"We're trying to get him discharged. He doesn't want any more treatment. All he wants is to go home. We're waiting on the doctors. They're having a hard time accepting it. All we can do is help make him comfortable."

"Is there anything I can do?"

Many people asked, and I always had the same answer: "Thank you, but I don't know what it would be."

If something needed doing, it was done. But so little could be done the helplessness nagged me constantly. Yet I knew that the angels sent help in all kinds of surprising ways.

"Well, his mouth is dry," I said, as we entered the room. "He really can't swallow anything or it triggers the pancreatic pain. We're using washcloths and a few ice chips."

Ed wet a fresh washcloth. "Mind if I take over, Jim?" He

handed the washcloth to Jimmy to suck on. "I was thinking, driving over, about the great times we had down at the lake."

Ed offered Jimmy a few ice chips on a spoon. Jimmy opened his mouth, let the ice dissolve on Jimmy's tongue.

"Remember that year you got sunburned?" Ed asked. "We couldn't get you off Boyd's water skis all afternoon. You kept tugging at the red around your bikini line. Boyd kept yelling at you to take it off. When you finally did, we all cheered." Ed rinsed the washcloth, moistened Jimmy's lips. "Remember that year you gave me a hard time when I said the clouds looked like body parts?"

Ed wanted so much to cheer him. But even a tiny smile was too far out of reach. Jimmy knew Ed would make it to this year's party and that he would never be going back. The lake was a lifetime away.

"We could always count on your raspberry pie to top off the beach dinner. It was like something out of *Sunset* magazine, Jimmy. Absolutely decadent."

I left them alone sharing "lake stories," hoping Ed could bring a smile to Jimmy's face.

I took a few minutes to stretch and walk around. When I went back in, Ed was saying: "...and then compulsive Willie started cleaning up around the bonfire. You know Willie. He had to have a roaring blaze. Before Gary could stop him, Willie tossed in what he thought was a sack of trash. People ducked behind towels. Ran for cover when the fireworks in the bag started going off."

Ed wanted so much to see Jimmy laugh, but Jimmy just couldn't. The sadness showed on both their faces.

They were quiet a few minutes, then Ed said, excitedly, "I'll be right back. Now don't you go anywhere."

Ed disappeared out the door. He flew back into the room about half an hour later with a brown paper bag in his hand.

He opened it next to Jimmy. "I had to go to the cosmetic department at Dillard's to get it," Ed said, and with a fanfare, "Ta-da!" pulled out a small, jet-black spray bottle.

Jimmy rolled his eyes at Ed.

Ed laughed, and added: "The sales clerk looked at me funny when I told her I wanted one like the kind used to set make-up. I didn't explain. You would have loved it."

Ed filled the bottle with tap water. Tested the flow of the spray on his hand before coming over to Jimmy. "Open your mouth a second, Jim. See if this helps."

Ed misted a few quick sprays of water in Jimmy's mouth. Jimmy swallowed, nodded, "Thanks, Ed."

We used that little spray bottle to moisten the inside of Jimmy's mouth for what turned out to be the rest of his life.

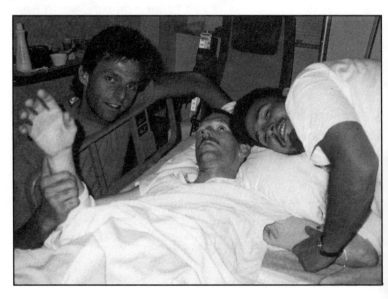

Ed, Jimmy, Kenny

On Giving Up

I remember going over to Libby's house, she on her sofa with her feet tucked under her, me in the rocking chair, knowing she would give me her time, quietly listen, without judgement, for as long as I needed. I started with the latest facts about Jimmy's health, just passing on the news. She asked me how I felt about that, and I knew it was safe to let my fears surface. I remember staring at the floor, rocking harder and faster, letting the tears and the screams come out: "My God, Libby. How am I going to live through this?"

Instead of accusing me of letting my feelings control me, she asked, "Can I hug you?"

"Please," I sobbed. "Oh, please, yes," feeling the deepest grief I'd ever felt.

She hugged me and she let me cry, knowing I had the choice to either feel my feelings, or run away from them. I chose my feelings: "It's AIDS. He's going to die. And *how* is he going to die? This can't be real!"

There were no words of comfort. Nothing that could be said, or needed to be said. I just needed to cry.

♥

"Florence, have you got a minute?" I asked. "Is this a good time to call?"

"What is it, Bobbie?"

"I'm feeling real scared, that's all."

"Can you tell me?"

"It's… It's everything."

"How's Jimmy?"

"They don't know what's going on with him. He can't hold anything in his stomach. They don't know why his temperature is going up and down. And I just had a fight with a doctor. They said if I wasn't happy with the care he was getting they'd move him to another hospital. They made it sound like a threat."

Florence asked, softly, "What can I do?"

"I think I just need to cry." I hung on to the phone with one hand, grabbed my belly with the other and sobbed and let loose the reservoir of tears that fear and anger had been holding down. I let it out… let it out… feeling my breath full for the first time in weeks… until… finally… the tears passed.

"Thank you, Florence. For picking up the phone."

"Anytime. Day or night. I'm here."

"I'm okay now."

"I know you are, Bobbie."

"I guess I'll go pick up Jimmy's prescription now."

♥

"Pat, there's got to be something else I can do for him."

"What would it be, Bobbie?"

"Maybe we could take him to Mexico or something."

"Does Jimmy want that?" she asked.

"When I mentioned it he shook his head and said, 'That's not for me.' I know he's right. But there must be a way to fight this. I'm losing him, Pat. He's not getting any better."

"He's doing this his way, Bobbie."

"But what if he dies? How can I just stand by?"

"Remember when you found that macrobiotic cookbook? And bought all that food and fixed those meals for him?"

"Jimmy hated it," I said, laughing through the tears. "When he tried it, he said he'd rather die than eat that stuff."

"Can you let him do it his way?"

"But what if he dies? What will I do?"

"Exactly what you're doing. Feel the anger and grief."

"This is horrible, Pat. Just horrible." I buried my head in her shoulder. And cried.

Pat, Jimmy, Florence

———————————— ♥ ————————————

I knew I wasn't big enough, strong enough, or smart enough to fight AIDS by myself. And I thanked God I didn't have to. I knew it was time to pull in all of my resources, and any and all resources the community had to offer. I prayed for strength and courage and help, and then I did the leg work necessary to find where help was available.

Before Jimmy became eligible for home care, before "The System" kicked in, Frank and I needed someone to be with Jimmy so we could take a break, slip away to a movie and try not to think about AIDS for a few hours.

Jimmy, of course, resisted: "I'm not a child, Mom. I don't want a stranger coming over here to baby-sit me. You guys go on to the movie. I'll be okay."

I said: "Honey, I know you don't feel right about this, but we have to do this for us. Having someone with you is the only way we can feel at ease about being away from you." What I didn't say was: *What if you have a seizure while we're away?*

We'd heard about the Metropolitan Community Church, an inter-denominational congregation where gays could worship together without threats of going to hell. The MCC had a volunteer group called SHARE, an AIDS love-care support team. Thank God they were there for us.

They sent Marshall. He knocked on our door one Sunday afternoon — tall, slender, gentle, compassionate, in his early forties and greying at the temples, with a soft Texas accent.

"Thanks for coming on such short notice," I said.

"Not at all. My pleasure. When they gave me his name it sounded familiar."

"He's back here."

When Jimmy saw him, they realized they had met before. They'd danced one time at *The Sŏc'* and the discomfort of having a stranger with him turned to relief. Marshall was an angel. We left hearing them laughing and talking about people they both knew.

♥

One night Jimmy said in desperate fear: "I've got to hear how other people deal with this. Someone who has AIDS."

He called the NMAPLA hotline (New Mexico Association for Persons Living with AIDS). Alonzo was the volunteer who answered the phone. They talked for more than an hour. He invited Jimmy to his home for dinner. Alonzo shared love, acceptance and understanding with Jimmy. Jimmy returned home that night with renewed hope, and an inner knowingness that he could cope, one day at a time, with his life. The terror was absent. He slept well that night. So did we.

♥

Frank and I could share our grief, but we needed a safe place to express our rage and not dump it on each other. We were desperate to learn how other people coped. I contacted New Mexico AIDS Services (NMAS) and learned about an ongoing, no fee, support group for "significant others of persons with AIDS." Frank and I went every Thursday night for more than a year and a half until Jimmy died.

The group sat around a table in the dining hall of a gentle little Episcopal church. There were parents at the table, lovers, dear friends. One mother had a son and a daughter and two grandchildren with AIDS. Some returned week after week. Others came once or twice and were never seen again. But those of us who continued shared our terror, our rage, our laughter, our grief, our gratitude with the group. We formed a unique bond over the months as we listened to each other, developed trusting, open hearts as we witnessed the ways we were living with AIDS and how AIDS was a part of our lives.

The group was a safe place to talk about, cry about, yell about the doctors, the treatments, the money, the prejudice, the friends and family who wouldn't come around, who never called, who only blamed, whose fears and judgements kept them away. We shared the helplessness of watching our loved one slowly die from this devastating disease and not be able to do a thing about it.

We learned about denial — blessed denial — and recognized our own denial more clearly when we saw it mirrored in others. We learned about the stages of the disease and of dying. About how each of us, not only the person dying, but each of us moved in and out of denial and isolation into anger, bargaining, depression, and finally, hopefully, acceptance. Rage changed to sadness, to loss, to tears at the hands dealt our loved ones. We watched people get stuck in one or another of those stages, disappear from the group and never return.

We learned loving a person with AIDS is everything. We couldn't cure them. Or keep them from dying. All we could do was love them. Unconditionally.

In one of the last groups we attended before Jimmy died, Frank and I shared our reality of letting Jimmy go. Another group member challenged us out of the different stage he was in at the time.

He shouted: "*My* son is strong! I know we can beat this thing."

It hurt to hear that he thought Jimmy was not strong, that he was weak, and that's why Jimmy would die.

Frank said, "It doesn't have anything to do with how strong you or anybody else thinks someone who has AIDS is. AIDS is a terminal disease."

"But you *can't* give up hope. You can *never* give up hope. He'll *die* if you give up!"

"There's a difference between giving up and letting go," Frank said.

"We're not giving up on love," I said. "We're letting go of trying to keep him alive. Of pretending to be God."

Frank added: "Our hope is he'll die a peaceful death. The way he wants to. Surrounded by people who love him."

Forgiveness

"I think about him when I'm by myself, when I'm driving to work, or watering the lawn."

* * *

"How do I tell him how much I care?"

* * *

"I never understood Jimmy, but I accept him for who he is. And I want to love him the way he is."

* * *

"The kids in school gave him a hard time. I didn't support him then, but I want to support him now."

* * *

"None of that matters anymore. All that matters is Jimmy."

* * *

"I'm so glad he told you. He's been so scared."

* * *

"Do we drop the ego and make a connection? Or waste what little time we have left?"

* * *

"There isn't time for pettiness. There's a 26-year-old in there dying."

* * *

"Does it matter that he was in the band instead of in football?"

* * *

"I'm sorry for the time we didn't spend together."

* * *

"Don't let guilt hang in the way. Be open."

* * *

"If you love him, tell him you do."

Families can be difficult to blend. Ours was no different, before AIDS. Before AIDS we thought we had years to reconcile our differences and to accept one another for who we were, plenty of time to let go of the painful past and to see each other without jealousy or resentment.

AIDS changed all that. A young life was sparking away before us. A son, a stepson, a brother, a half-brother, a grandson, a nephew, an uncle yet to be, a friend would soon be out of our sight, out of our hearing, out of our touch forever. Those of us who kept our hearts open by expressing our fears, crying our tears, listening to each other, talking about the moment instead of the weather, those of us who chose to walk that dark, scary path found light and love awaiting us.

With Jimmy's physical deterioration came a flowering of his spiritual being, the part of him greater than his body. And we marveled at his unique orchestration of what was his journey home. Whenever he mentioned anyone's name, I encouraged him to call, believing he must have a need to shed old hurt and to say, "Goodbye."

"I wonder how Ted's doing," Jimmy said late one night. The house was quiet. Frank was sleeping. I was waiting up with Jimmy, waiting for the nurse to arrive.

"You want to give him a call and find out?"

Jimmy's relationship with Ted in St. Louis was brief and fiery. I knew they loved each other the best way they knew how, until fear and fatigue separated them in heartache and confusion shortly before Jimmy moved back to Albuquerque.

Ted could have been like a son-in-law to me. It was easy for us to talk. Ted was intelligent, had gone through several of the Twelve-Step programs, seemed open, knew how to talk about feelings.

I had a lot of hopes for that relationship. It seemed a most romantic thing for Jimmy to have the equivalent of a marriage, to have somebody care for him in a spousal way. Like John E. and John M. connecting when they both had AIDS. Like Matt and Bobby trying so hard to make it work.

Jimmy and Ted were in St. Louis. If the relationship worked, Jimmy would stay in St. Louis with Ted caring for him, and me only visiting. But if the relationship didn't work, Jimmy would move back to Albuquerque and I could care for him. I was torn between my hopes for the success of the relationship and my selfishness of wanting Jimmy close to home.

I knew watching Jimmy die would be the hardest, the most painful thing I would ever do. Yes, it would be hard. Yes, it would hurt. But it was my only chance to do it. There's not a chance to feel the love if there's not a warm body there to exchange it.

When I heard Jimmy say, "We had to break up, Ted just can't do it," my attitude then was: *Fuck that! He won't do it!*

He's afraid of the pain! We're doing it. There's nothing different about us! It hurts us too! Don't give me "He can't." He won't!

I had a lot of judgement about all of that. That's where I was then. I saw it as a selfish decision Ted was making, not a disability. My anger and resentment helped sustain me day-to-day. I knew I wouldn't die from AIDS and I knew Frank wouldn't. What I didn't know was that more than half of Jimmy's friends would.

I can say now, "Maybe some people just can't."

Every friend who came through was a connection for me with Jimmy. I'd think: *What a nice guy this is. I can see why Jimmy and he are friends.* I saw a bigger picture of Jimmy through his friends. That's the gift his friends gave me. The ones who stopped seeing Jimmy stopped seeing me, too. Losing a friend of Jimmy's was like losing a part of Jimmy too.

I knew there was something unique every person who came through the door, every person who called, was sharing. I knew the experience would change our lives forever. We were moving through something that would bond us. Maybe we'd met only a time or two, but we went through Jimmy's dying process together. Like Jimmy's friend Rick, the potter from Santa Fe. He came to the house, spent time with Jimmy, wrote two beautiful letters. All I did was open the door for Rick, give him a hug, say goodbye when he left. But now he's remembered. He was part of the process. Rick did what he could do.

As the years go by, I've become less and less "Jimmy's mother" and more a friend. I've found out even more about why Jimmy liked these people, why they liked Jimmy. They feel free to share stories with me: "You know, Bobbie, I never did tell you this about Jimmy, but now I feel I can." I hang on to those stories: "Oh, good! Tell me more!"

Look what families cut themselves off from when they cut themselves off from their son's friends. Tim's family. Bobby's family. Fergie's family. That's a part of him they'll *never* know if they don't know his gay friends.

Jimmy said: "I wouldn't know how to get hold of Ted. I threw away his number."

"I still have it." I saved all the phone numbers I had of Jimmy's friends.

"You do?!"

"I'll get him on the phone if you want to talk to him."

Jimmy said, shaking his head, "I can't believe you kept his number, Mom." Then, "I don't know what I'd say."

I asked my angels to talk to his angels and to, *Please, show him what he needs to say.*

"What do you want him to know?" I asked.

Jimmy was quiet a few moments.

"Honey, you loved each other. Whatever happened between you two, that love doesn't die."

He took a deep breath, let it out and said, "Go ahead and call."

I did: "Ted, this is Bobbie in Albuquerque. Jimmy wants to talk to you."

I handed the phone to Jimmy. "Here he is, Honey." His eyes were on mine, questioning. I nodded, "It's okay."

Jimmy's eyes softened. He took the phone and said: "I'm sick, Ted. I'm dying. I just want to tell you… " (the tears were coming) " …I need to let you know… I forgive you…. I forgive myself for all that happened between us…. I don't want to take that pain with me…. I… love… you…. Goodbye."

Love

A Gathering

One by one, over what turned out to be the last few weeks of his life, Jimmy personally invited the people he wanted to be near him when he died.

"Stasey, I'd really like you to be here. Would you?"

"Sure, Bro. Whatever you want."

"Dik, I'd like you to be with me when I die."

"I'd love to. Do you have any idea when that will be?"

"Oh, in about a year," Jimmy answered.

"Okay. Well, then, I'll go on to Spain."

I had no idea when Jimmy would die. No one did. I wanted to fulfill his wishes, but wondered how that could possibly happen. Half of the people lived out-of-state. There'd be last-minute plane reservations, emergency leave from work. Logistically, it didn't seem possible to gather all of them around the bed as Jimmy let out his last breath.

Then one morning, the nurse's aide assigned to the night shift joined me in the kitchen. I was standing at the table folding clothes. I signed his time sheet, acknowledging the hours he sat with Jimmy, and returned to folding a towel.

He thanked me and said: "You know, no one can predict when someone will die. But I've cared for a lot of people who are dying, and one thing I've noticed. There's a change in their breathing pattern toward the end."

I stopped folding, sat down and listened to him.

"There's been a noticeable shift in Jim's breathing," he continued, "just in the few days I've been here. To what I've seen in the others."

"What do you mean?"

"Well, he'll take a breath and then there'll be a long time before he breathes again."

"So…. "

"I've timed it. The space between his breaths is getting longer. It's been my experience that the patient dies within seven to ten days after this shift in breathing. Of course," he added hurriedly, "there are exceptions…." in a voice that sounded very far away.

Seven to ten days?! my mind screamed. *Do I need to call the people on Jimmy's list? What will they think? Will they rush over here? Are the angels letting me know something only they can know? After all, no doctor will predict how long Jimmy has. But then, what if Jimmy dies without the people he wants with him? How will I live with myself?*

But how could I tell Jimmy he might have only a week left to live? My God, how could I? How could I bear to see panic in his eyes?

I asked my angels: *Please help me be as gentle as I can. Help me with the words.*

I heard: *We'll help. You'll know.*

I went in to see him. "Good morning, Sunshine. How're you feeling today?"

"I'm not sure," he said, distracted.

"Oh?" He looked the same as yesterday, his color pale but

normal, a few dozen hairs loose on his pillow, his eyes staring but clear. I busied myself with the vase of flowers by his bed. "Looks like these roses are just about spent," I said, picking a dead blossom off the stem. "Weren't these the most perfect white roses you've ever seen?"

"Mom," he said. "I just had the most real dream I've ever had." He took a sip of water, rubbed the sleep out of his eyes. "I was talking to Jamie. There were lots of other people around too. Timmy. And Bruce. And lots of light."

Oh, my God! Those people are dead! They're already talking to him! Can this be real?

Yes, the angels answered. *It's real.*

· I stopped rearranging the flowers. "You know, Honey, how you were telling me who you want with you when you die?"

"Yes?" he asked, still dreamy, still in that other world.

"I've been thinking," I said, hesitating, trying to delay telling him what the nurse's aide said about his breathing. "You've asked all these people to be with you. And they want to be with you too, Jimmy. But, how do you see that happening?"

"Well. I'd like to… I want to hear what they have to say to me. I want us to be able to say goodbye."

"Honey, you've got to be alive to do that."

"Yeah. So. What's your point?"

"Jimmy, there's just no way of knowing what's going to happen. You could trip and hit your head and die tomorrow. What if something did happen? And you didn't get to have those people here?"

He was deep in thought, slowly twirling the ends of his mustache. "I see what you're saying. Maybe you're right."

"I don't want to scare you, Honey, but... "

"You know, I wonder if Stasey would want to come out for his birthday. I'd like to see him."

"That's next week."

"We could have everyone here. It'll be fine, Mom. Really. Go ahead and call."

His Last Haircut

Friday, August 25th

It was the day before Stasey's birthday. Three days before Jimmy died.

Cathy and Kandi were the first to arrive. They came with their mother, Jimmy's step-grandmother, who everyone called Mee-Ma. Stasey and his wife Mary were due early tomorrow. Buddy and Ophelia by tomorrow afternoon.

It was just before dinner. We were all in Jimmy's room. Jimmy asked, "Did you bring your scissors, Aunt Cathy?"

"I always have them with me, Jimmy. Why? Do you want your hair cut?"

"Yes, I do."

"We'll do it sometime. Before everyone else gets here."

"No. I want you to cut it *now*."

Surprised glances passed among us.

Cathy said: "All right, Jimmy. You're the boss."

"We can use that wheelchair. You guys sit me up in it. Stuff pillows between me and the sides to support me so I don't fall. And drape a sheet around me. I don't want itchy, loose hairs all over me."

He was already throwing back the cotton blanket. This was a different Jimmy I was seeing. Determined. Taking charge. It was wonderful.

And it scared the hell out of me.

Cathy had an arm under one leg, Kandi an arm under his other leg. They locked their other arms around his back, forming a chair. "On three," Jimmy said.

Mee-Ma said: "Be careful with him. Don't drop him."

The nurse locked the brakes on the wheelchair, guided him in, arranged the pillows. He was safely in the chair. It was time to leave them alone.

I said: "Honey, Pat's invited me and Frank to her birthday party. But this looks like more fun. If you'd rather we stay here… "

"No," he said. "You'll see the finished product when you get back. I'm ready, Aunt Cathy. Let's get clipping."

"Are you sure you trust me with these scissors, Jimmy?" Cathy said, getting the scissors out of her purse.

"Sure I do," Jimmy said. "But get the hand mirror out of the bathroom, I want to watch. See you later, Mom. Give Pat a birthday hug for me."

He was sitting up in the wheelchair with a sheet draped completely around him, from his neck all the way down to the floor. Cathy had the scissors in her hand, snipping away. They were laughing and talking. The back of his head was toward me. I couldn't see his receding hairline, how old his thinning hair made him appear. From here, he didn't look sick at all.

I went over to him, kissed his cheek. "Goodbye," I said. "I love you."

I checked the butterfly bandage taped to his forehead where he'd fallen in the bathroom the day before, noticed the old scar on his upper lip showing through his mustache. When he was three years old he'd tripped in day-care and hit the corner of a table. His mustache had been so thick....

He gave me a smile. "I love you too, Mom. Aunt Cathy, I want a little off the sides. Not too much off the top. And my sideburns to here."

I said, "I can see you're in charge, Jimmy."

"Goodbye, Mom," he said.

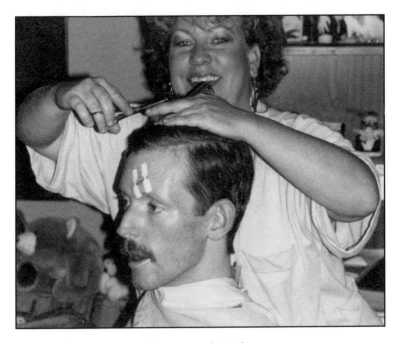

Jimmy and Cathy

When Frank and I got to Pat and Tom's, the party was in full bloom, the room full of life. We stood off to the side with our backs against the wall. It was Pat's 40th birthday. She said the theme was to honor the child in each of us. Balloons and children's games were spread around the room. The refreshments were red punch and chocolate-chip cookies.

We watched Pat's friends line up, blindfolded, to play Pin-the-Tail-on-the-Donkey, a game Jimmy and Stasey used to play when they were kids, with Kandi. She had baby-sat the boys when they went to live with Buddy and Ophelia. It was her summer job in high school. I remember Kandi telling me that she always knew Jimmy was different, and she loved him even more because of it. Now twenty years later, she was helping her sister give Jimmy a haircut, possibly his last, while not ten feet away from me, healthy people were socializing, spending an evening celebrating.

How can they be living normal lives? Don't they know my son is dying?

"Frank, take me home," I said. "I have to get out of here."

Pat and Tom understood. They thanked us for staying as long as we did.

When Frank and I got in the car, my God, *didn't the tears come.*

"When will our lives be normal again?" I cried. "Does Jimmy have to die for that to happen? Those people, Frank, they have no idea what we're going through."

Frank said, "How can they?"

"I want it to be over with," I said. Then: "What am I saying? I don't want it over. Frank, I'm scared he's close."

"Yes, I think he is," Frank said as he parked at the curb on the street in front of our home.

"I need another minute. I can't go back in crying like this."

"What can I do, Bobbie?"

"Hold me. Please, just hold me."

Finally I said: "Okay. I'm ready. Now I can go in."

We walked in, walked back towards Jimmy's room. Cathy met us in the hallway.

She said: "I'm glad you're back. I got his hair cut. We got him back in bed. Everything was just fine. Then he had a seizure. He's been like this ever since."

Coming Together

The Next Morning

Stasey and I were in the room with Jimmy, along with Mary, Peter, and Laura. Laura was taking his vital signs. She said, "That incident last night must have been a TIA."

Stasey asked, "How are you now, Jim?"

"Okay," Jimmy said.

He was in bed, his cotton thermal blanket loose over his legs.

Jimmy, Stasey, Mary

Jimmy said, "Mom, would you get that white box down from the closet?"

I handed the box to Jimmy. Jimmy took it, held it a second, handed it to Stasey and said, "Happy birthday."

Stasey opened it. "Your hat. Your cowboy hat."

"I want you to have it," Jimmy said.

It was a birthday present, but it was the last present Stasey would ever receive from Jimmy. They both knew it. Their eyes said more than words could possibly tell.

Stasey ran his fingers around the felt brim. "I've always liked this hat on you, Jim." Then holding it by the crown, he ducked his head and slipped it on.

Jimmy nodded, "It looks real good on you, Stasey."

Stasey's eyes met Jimmy's eyes, turned red and wet and he said, "I'll sure take good care of it." And he wiped at a tear.

A silence filled the room. Peter asked, "Do you want us to leave?"

Jimmy said, "No, you guys can stay." And to Mary he said, "Take good care of him, Mary."

She slipped her hand in Stasey's. "I will," she said. "I promise."

Mary was Stasey's anchor. I knew she would encourage him to feel his grief. Stasey would be all right.

Together they left the room.

"Jimmy," I said. "Stasey and Mary and Frank and I are taking a quick trip to the mountain this morning. Frank wants to shoot a video up there so you can see the property."

"Sure. Go ahead. I'll be okay."

Frank and I had purchased the property just 5½ weeks before. We'd always wanted a place in the mountains where the kids could go. Jimmy had never seen it. We wanted him to see it, to know how peaceful the mountain felt.

But Jimmy didn't seem interested in this mission that felt so important to us.

I kissed his cheek. "We'll be back about the same time everyone else gets here."

On our way out, we ran into Buddy and Ophelia coming up the driveway. Frank put the video camera down, gave Buddy a hug, said, "We're doing a turn-around trip to the mountain to shoot a video for Jimmy. We'll watch it together tonight."

Buddy said, "We'll be here."

Ophelia had an armful of sunshine-yellow gladiolus. She said, "We stopped by the Silver Petal on the way over for these. Aren't they beautiful?"

"They are," I said. "Jimmy will love them."

She said: "Oh, Cathy and Kandi are still at the motel. They said that after breakfast, they'd be picking up more white candles."

"Good," I said. "Everyone should be here by two p.m."

"You all take your time, now. Don't worry about a thing. We'll do whatever needs doing."

We piled into the Wagoneer, Frank and I in the front seat, Stasey and Mary in the back. We drove the hour and forty-five minutes mostly in silence. I don't know what everyone else was thinking in the quiet, but I was praying: *God, please don't let him die before we get back. Please help us show him this beautiful mountain the only way we know how.*

When we got there, the sky was that clear, deep, high-altitude blue, not a cloud anywhere in sight. We parked the car, climbed the trail through the Ponderosa pines to the aspen grove at the top of the hill.

Stasey looked so comfortable in his safari shorts, white polo shirt, and Jimmy's cowboy hat, now his hat. I asked him if he was cold. He said, "No." I said, "I am." I had on Jimmy's orange turtleneck, his long-sleeved flannel shirt with the blue St. Bernards printed on it, and the khaki windbreaker Jimmy borrowed from Rob and Rob let him keep. Mary was wearing loose walking shorts, white sneakers, and a heavy knit sweater over an identical orange turtleneck that she and Jimmy bought together the same day at Spectrum's. Frank had on his regular Saturday shirt.

Frank pointed to Sandia Crest, a hazy fifty miles away, barely visible through a notch in the far hills. He pointed to Redondo Peak, five miles away, paused a few moments, looked around. "There may be prettier places in the world," he said, "but I don't know where. Jim's going to love it here."

Every step taken, every wildflower pointed out, every word softly spoken, was with Jimmy in mind. He would never feel the crisp breeze blowing off the mountaintop, or the early morning sun shining warm on his face. He would never hear the bugling of the elk, or smell the pine sap dripping off the trees. And we all knew it as we made our way slowly downhill to the rocks at the base of the property.

"The rocks look like a family," Mary said.

"That one looks just like an armchair."

Frank brushed the pine needles from its seat, sat down, and asked, "Care to try it?"

We took turns. Marveled at how comfortable the hard rock could be.

Then we sat in front of the video camera, and each of us talked to Jimmy:

"This sure is a beautiful spot, Jim."

"I want to tell you how grateful I am to you for deciding to let us bring your remains up here. I know you know how much it's going to mean to us. I love you with all of my heart and with all of this mountain and with all of my soul."

"Jim, I really wish you could be up here. But you've got such important things to do at this time. And you've been so brave through all of this. Thank you for letting me see what you've been going through. It's meant so much to me. I love you very much."

"Jim, you're one of the reasons we bought this place. I know both of us were thinking about you when we did. Now any of the family who wants to, can come up here and spend time. Camp out. Be with you. You'll love it here, Jim."

"Well, Jim. It's going to be real hard. For me to say goodbye. But this will be a place where I can come, and come visit you. It's such a beautiful spot. It's, ah… you're going to love it here. I love you very much."

Frank shut off the camera, re-wound the tape, and we headed off the mountain back home.

On the drive back, Mary said, "Every time Jimmy's been hospitalized or taken a turn for the worse, it's been on a weekend."

"Today's Saturday," someone said.

"There's no way Jimmy would die on Stasey's birthday," I said. "He just wouldn't do it."

When we pulled into the driveway, there was Buddy and Ophelia's car, Mee-Ma's car, Rob's brown Saab (I flashed on the red velvet Christmas bow Jimmy had made and hung on the front of it when he picked Rob up from the airport last Christmas). Among the cars parked in the street, I recognized Peter's "it's-beat-up-but-it-gets-me-there" car. And parked right behind my Volvo was Mother's car. It's been hard for her to be here. Six month's ago her granddaughter Jamie died, and now Jimmy. Mother looked numb the times she could be here.

I turned the key in the door, pushed it open, Stasey, Mary and Frank right behind. Mary said, "Looks like a party going on."

I hoped so.

There was Scarlett, wagging her tail and rooting her nose, smelling mountain smells on our clothes.

"Hello, girl," I said. "You look pretty excited. Everything okay?" I dropped to my knees and rubbed her thick, Shepherd neck. She spun away and ran down the hall.

Mee-Ma came around the corner from the kitchen carrying a tray of sandwiches and a pitcher of iced tea, headed toward the patio.

"Let me get that for you, Mee-Ma," Stasey said as he opened the screen door. I heard Stasey greet the people on the deck: "Howdy. How're you all doing?"

I peeked out, waved to the group outside. They were standing, sitting, visiting with each other, listening to the water trickle over the fountain Frank worked day and night to complete.... *God, was that only six weeks ago?*

I headed on back to Jimmy's room. Laura and Ophelia were smiling and talking just outside Jimmy's open door.

"Hi, Bobbie," Laura said. "Jimmy seems to be comfortable. He can't talk much, but he says a lot with those eyes."

I looked in the room to let Jimmy know we were back. Rob was sitting on the chair closest to the bed, leaning near Jimmy, holding his hands. Rob was talking, Jimmy listening. I didn't go in.

I went back into the kitchen, sat down, and breathed a sigh of relief. Everything was being taken care of.

Thank you, angels. For bringing us together.

I thought of a friend of Jimmy's who had stopped coming around and decided to phone him: "I just want to let you know what Jimmy's situation is. Give you a chance to see him. He might not have much longer."

"Bobbie, I can't. I'm sorry, I just can't."

"Okay," I said. "Jimmy seems to understand. I just wanted to let you know."

Every effort was made for everyone to be together who could and wanted to. There was every opportunity in between group gatherings for private visits. I felt like I was driven to give his friends a chance to be with him, to give him a chance to be with his friends.

I learned through Jimmy that he and his friends had an ability to let go of painful pasts. Whatever had happened between them, whatever the reason they weren't together now, none of that mattered. This was a tremendous lesson for me in acceptance and forgiveness.

Ophelia joined me in the kitchen. I said, "I can't tell you how good it is to have you here."

"I wouldn't want to be anywhere else," she said. "I got to thinking about our time with him. I had him thirteen years, and... "

"And I had him thirteen years," I said. "I just figured that out this morning, myself!"

And we hugged each other. And laughed.

"He's been lucky to have you."

"We've been lucky to have him."

Mee-Ma came scurrying in from the laundry room with

a freshly-folded stack of clean towels. Kandi stuck her head in the kitchen. "It's two o'clock," she said. "Everyone's here who's going to be here. I think Jimmy might be getting tired. Do you want to get started?"

We crowded into Jimmy's room, gathered around his bed. I noticed the yellow glads bursting out of the crystal vase in the corner, how nicely Ophelia had arranged them, and that someone, probably Rob, had brought more Stargazer lilies. White candles were everywhere: on the drop desk, the end table, his bedside table, on top of the TV, even the window sills. They were all lit now. Through the window the gentle sound of the waterfall could be heard, just outside, on the patio. Soothing. Constant.

"Let's hold hands," I said, taking one of Jimmy's hands. Jimmy took Stasey's hand, who took Buddy's, then around the bed, Mee-Ma and Cathy and Mary and Frank and Laura and Petey and Rob and Steve-O and Bobby and Matt and Peter and Kandi until Ophelia took my hand completing the circle. "I want to thank all our angels for bringing us together."

We took a minute and breathed together. In silence.

Then we prayed: "Dear God. We know you hold Jimmy in your arms. Your loving arms. You always have and we know you are now. You've brought so much love in and around all of us, through Jimmy. We are grateful for your incredible gifts of love. Amen."

People echoed: "Amen."

We squeezed hands.

"Thanks, everyone," Jimmy said. "I couldn't have done it without you."

During the late-afternoon lull, the house quiet again, Frank asked Jimmy if he was ready to watch the video.

Frank said: "We can move the mattress and your pillows into the living room. Stasey and I can pick you up, carry you out there. So you can see it on the big screen."

"I don't think I'm up to it just now."

"We'll make you comfortable, Jim. I promise."

"No. I don't want to move out of my room."

He never saw the video of the forest where his ashes are right now.

"Ma - Ma"

By nine o'clock everyone had gone. Stasey, Mary, Frank and I were sitting at the kitchen table talking about the day. Jimmy lay in his bed sleeping, Laura watching him.

We heard Laura yell from the bedroom, "I need help in here!" Frank and Stasey ran ahead of me down the hall.

Laura had her hands full. Jimmy was trying to get up out of bed.

They were helping her now, Frank supporting his head, Stasey trying to keep the IV pole from toppling over, Laura clearing his mouth, all six hands trying to keep him from falling, from hurting himself. I heard someone say "projectile vomiting." And I heard another voice, Jimmy's voice, louder, stronger, forcing words out with every rasping breath.

"Ma-ma!" he was calling, "Ma-ma! Ma-ma!" over and over again, calling me to be with him as he died.

I didn't care about the vomit, I had to hold him. I climbed in bed with him, scooped him in my arms, put his head against my chest, rocked him, told him: "Mama's here. I'm right here, Honey. Mama's right here."

He kept calling: "Ma-ma! Ma-ma! Ma-ma! Ma-ma! Ma-ma! Ma-ma!"

It was like he was wide awake, but why couldn't he see me? Why couldn't he hear me? Why didn't he know I was there?

"Ma-ma! Ma-ma! Ma-ma! Ma-ma! Ma-ma! Ma-ma!"

He had to be dying. "Mama's right here, Honey. It's okay. You can let go now. Mama's here."

"Ma-ma! Ma-ma! Ma-ma! Ma-ma! Ma-ma! Ma-ma! Ma-ma! Ma-ma! Ma-ma! Ma-ma! Ma-ma!"

I held him. Rocked him. "It's okay, Jimmy. Mama loves you. Mama's here."

"Ma-ma! Ma-ma! Ma-ma! Ma-ma!"

"Mama's got you. You can let go now. You've done such a good job, Baby. You can go now. Look for the light."

But it didn't stop.

"Ma-ma! Ma-ma.... "

I held him. Rocked him.

With every breath he kept saying: "Ma-ma! Ma-ma! Ma-ma! Ma-ma! Ma-ma...! "

Every breath.

Every breath.

Every breath.

"Ma-ma! Ma-ma! Ma-ma!"

I just kept rocking him and telling him: "I'm right here. I'm right here, Honey. It's okay. You can go now. It's all right. Mama's here."

All those times I wasn't with him when he was a little boy. All those times he must have cried out: "Mama. Why did you leave me?"

He was crying *now* for all those times I wasn't there. For all those times... *I wasn't there.*

"Ma-ma! Ma-ma! Ma-ma! Ma-ma! Ma-ma! Ma-ma!

Ma-ma! Ma-ma! Ma-ma! Ma-ma! Ma-ma! Ma-ma!

I didn't want to turn loose of him.

He just kept crying my name over and over: "Ma-ma! Ma-ma! Ma-ma! Ma-ma! Ma-ma! Ma-ma!"

I don't know how long I held him like that. The nurse who relieved Laura said he was just making sounds, that he didn't know what he was saying. But I knew. It was my name he was calling. It was me.

Sometime, it seemed like hours later, Frank and Stasey pulled me away.

Stasey said: "You two try and get some sleep. I want to sit with him. I'll let you know if there's a change."

I lay on my side, in bed, with the bedroom door open, not moving. Eyes wide. My body tired. Listening.

With every breath: "Ma-ma. Ma-ma. Ma-ma. Ma-ma. Ma-ma."

With every breath.

Every breath.

"Ma-ma. Ma-ma. Ma-ma. Ma-ma. Ma-ma...."

During the dark early morning hours, his breathing got slower. He couldn't say the M's anymore. The words became sounds, just: "Ah... ah. Ah... ah."

"Ah..." on the in-breath, "ah...." on the out-breath.

"Ah..." in breath, "ah...." out breath.

"Ah... ah.... Ah... ah.... Ah... ah.... Ah... ah.... Ah... ah.... Ah... ah.... Ah... ah.... Ah... ah.... Ah... ah...." quieter and quieter.

Then there was no sound on the in-breath.

Only "... ...ah. ... ...ah. ... ...ah. ... ...ah. ... ...ah. ... ...ah. ... ... ah...." until it was no more than a quiet murmur. And it was Sunday morning light.

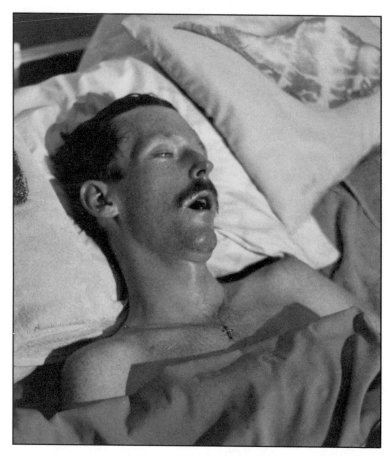

Jimmy

He stayed in a quiet coma all day Sunday, Sunday night, and Monday morning.

Jim E. Mitchell died at 1:10 p.m., Monday afternoon, August 28, 1989.

What fine work my son did.

The Mountain
Labor Day, 1989

The memorial service was over. Only family were left to pick up the flowers and gather the photographs of Jimmy, all of us quietly helping to leave the church as we'd found it. Passing from the meeting hall to the sanctuary, I saw Buddy standing in the back corner, his hands pushed deep in his suit pockets. He was looking up towards the altar staring at Jimmy's portrait with tears in his eyes.

As I approached Buddy, a quiet space of privateness surrounded us. His eyes tore themselves away from the altar and met mine. I took another step toward him, let my arms slowly open, saw Buddy's arms mirror mine. I felt Jimmy's presence surround us. We embraced.

For the first time, we let ourselves feel what price we'd paid to have Jimmy in our lives.

We cried, both of us, Jimmy's parents, as we held each other in Jimmy's love. Jimmy's presence was so strong, I looked up, above and behind Buddy, expecting to see him there. A golden light filled a corner that had been dark.

After the memorial service, we loaded in cars, formed a caravan to the mountain. We stopped at the crematorium to pick up Jimmy's ashes. Frank and I went in, requested the remains of Jim E. Mitchell. The man disappeared down the hallway and we waited for him to return with our son's body.

He came back carrying a simple, brown, cardboard box 8x8x10½ inches. He set it on the countertop. Frank signed the papers. I put my arms around the box. And cried.

Frank stopped at a 7-Eleven, bought brown paper bags and a plastic scoop. When we got to our property, he placed them and Jimmy's box on the picnic table. We stood staring at the box, waiting for someone to open it.

A swarm of bees droned all around the picnic table. They landed on my hands, on my cheeks, as if kissing me. The bees were on my face, on my upper lip, all over the brim of the hat, Jimmy's hat, that I was wearing. They crawled on my fingertips as I carefully opened the box.

No one swatted. No one ran. We each took a sack, and one by one, we scooped ashes into our little bags. Then we went our different directions to scatter, privately, where we wanted Jimmy to be: under a pine tree; the soil in a bed of wildflowers; in the grove of aspens; tossed to the four winds. I placed mine, each tiny fragment, in a crevice, at the base of a family of rocks.

We met again at the picnic table. The honeybees had disappeared. Frank lit a fire and we gathered around the fire pit, in a circle, held hands, listened as each of us said goodbye:

"Thank you, Jimmy. For showing us how to love."

"And for facing death with dignity and grace."

"There were many things we didn't agree on, Jim. But as time passed, the lines between us began to blur. I'll miss you, Jimmy. Thanks for being you."

"We learned a lot from each other, Bro. I love you."

"Peace be with you."

"Goodbye, Son."

"Goodbye, Jimmy."

"Goodbye, Jimmy."

"Goodbye."

We scattered handfuls of ashes in the firepit. Some of us cried. I knew I would be sitting there in years to come staring at the dancing firelight, thinking about him on quiet nights with the fire flickering toward the heavens and countless stars bright overhead.

I miss my son's body, but I embrace the love he left behind. I cannot touch his skin, look into his eyes, stroke his hair, hear his laughter, comfort his tears. All that is gone. What remains is in a cloudy glass vase on a mantle next to a photograph of him holding a baby. I lost my son's body, but we all found love.

God is love, and he that
dwelleth in love dwelleth in
God, and God in him.

- 1 John 4:16

Epilogue

His Ashes

Jimmy's ashes have been scattered around the world by friends wishing to honor his love of traveling.

Frank and I: in a stone crevice in Devil's Chair, on the Salisbury Plain in south-central England; in the River Ness below Inverness Castle in the Highlands of Scotland.

Dik: in Avila, Seville, and Olite, Spain; and in Florence, Italy, on the heads (and in the laps) of two handsome men rowing beneath the Ponte Vecchio over the river Arno.

Steve-O: in Livermore, Los Angeles, Golden Gate Park in San Francisco; out his car window on a warm, breezy day miles from nowhere in south Kansas; into the north wind over the rim of the Grand Canyon; "Jimmy's box" at the Cornell house in Albuquerque; on Farmer Street, 14th Street, and Wilson Street in Phoenix; mixed into the clay of some of Steve's sculptures; to places in Europe: Budapest, Sophia, Thessaloniki, the Trevi fountain in Rome, in Pisa, Aix-en-Provence, Grenoble, Paris, London and in the crypt below St. Stephen's Cathedral in Vienna. Steve wrote about that: *Below the Cathedral, there is a large, cool, very quiet crypt where the bones of thousands of Black Death victims are stacked. Since history will remember our time in the same way we remember the* great European plagues, Jimmy's ashes belong with those bones.

In the Pacific Equatorial Current on the waters off Costa Rica.

On a rocky prominence facing west from Madrid, New Mexico.

In a nuclear submarine somewhere under the North Atlantic.

On the waters of Hahn's Bay, North Dakota.

On the sand at Lyon's Beach at Elephant Butte Lake, Truth or Consequences, New Mexico.

Among the flowers of the International Peace Garden on the border of the United States and Canada.

Among the irises in a certain garden on 17th Street in Albuquerque.

We had asked his friends, if they wished, to memorialize Jim by planting a tree in celebration of his love of life.

Frank and Petey and Matt and Bobby and Ricardo and I planted three dwarf fruit trees in our backyard. Heavy with harvest, those trees have broken branches each summer since the year after Jimmy died.

Three mulberry trees were planted in the playground of a day-care for the children of homeless parents.

A silver maple in Bruce and Dolores' front yard.

A tender sapling in a reforestation program in the California Sierras.

A peach tree in J.W.'s backyard that bears the most delicious fruit we have ever tasted.

A Spanish broom in my sister's garden in Silver City, New Mexico.

And a tall shade tree in a public park in Albuquerque that children play under all year long.

Acknowledgements

To you who appeared in my life during the last months of Jimmy's journey Home: strangers who touched me, friends who listened, family who gathered close. I wish to honor each of you who participated in Jimmy's dying process. From the book's inception, I struggled with knowing not everyone could be mentioned in the writing. Please know you are not forgotten. I am eternally grateful.

To the gay community, warriors battling on the front lines and in the trenches against a powerful, deadly disease. Who have spent more than a decade establishing a network of support in the midst of their own personally devastating losses. Who have laid groundwork for the rest of us to find gentle, quiet help in a world that offers screaming condemnation to persons with AIDS, persons who continue to die, many judged, alienated and abandoned.

To my husband, Frank Stubbs, who remains steadfastly present offering himself as an anchor of love, support and understanding. Who held me and allowed me to walk through my pain while Jimmy was dying. Who unwaveringly supported me in the writing of this book even though to do so meant he, too, would remember and feel his own grief.

To my editor, Ed Dziczek, who early in its writing, recognized and respected the life and importance of the book. Who devoted his own time, talents and energy, encouraging me to continue writing when waves of overwhelm washed over me. Who understood the healing necessity of allowing me to write everything down, and then, just as healing and necessary, gently encouraged me to delete pages for the sake of the story.

To the beauty of everlasting friendships.

And to the healing love that lifts the veil of fear.